Carl Faelten

Boston Art Guide and Artists' Directory

Carl Faelten

Boston Art Guide and Artists' Directory

ISBN/EAN: 9783743317420

Manufactured in Europe, USA, Canada, Australia, Japa

Cover: Foto ©ninafisch / pixelio.de

Manufactured and distributed by brebook publishing software (www.brebook.com)

Carl Faelten

Boston Art Guide and Artists' Directory

BOSTON

ART GUIDE

AND

ARTISTS' DIRECTORY

Established 1810

Williams & Everett

Importers & Dealers in Paintings and Water Colors

Engravings, Etchings, &c. &c.

FRAMES FOR PORTRAITS, ENGRAVINGS AND MIRRORS A SPECIALTY.

An Exhibition of Fine Pictures, etc. Gallery open to Visitors.

190. Boylston St. Boston

PAINTED BY L. EM LE ADAN. ENGRAVED BY M. L. BROWN.

A SUMMER EVENING.

Preface

THIS Guide has been compiled for the purpose of serving those interested in the *Fine Arts* in this city and throughout the United States. By the term *Fine Arts*, we mean to include all the Graphic Arts, and the volume will show to what extent the Graphic Arts are practised in this city, and it will be of especial interest to those who are immediately interested in their growth and development.

The information contained in the Art Guide will be found accurate. Great care has been exercised in its preparation, and it has been the sole aim of the publishers to make the volume such that it can be implicitly relied on as a book of reference.

Special attention has been given to different exhibits throughout the United States, and to the various art educational institutions. The lists of names will be of service to those who are interested in art work, and will serve a commendable commercial purpose for all those who may have dealings with artists, architects, engravers, etc., and it is hoped that the volume will prove of value to all interested in art.

WHEAT PUBLISHING CO.
14 STATE STREET

Contents

Art Clubs.
Art Institutions of the United States.
Art Exhibitions, 1892-3.
Art Galleries.
Art Institutions and Collections.
Artists — Their Reception Days.
Art Schools.
Art Scholarship.
Architects.
Architectural Draughtsmen.
China Painters.
Crayon Portraits.
Flower Painters.
Illustrators and Designers.
Mechanical Draughtsmen.
Monuments — Names of Sculptors.
Sculptors.
Studios — Location.
Teachers.
The Law of Copyright.
The Tariff.
Trade List (Classified).

New England Conservatory of Music and Fine Arts.

Franklin Square, BOSTON, MASS.

Founded by Dr. E. TOURJEE.

CARL FAELTEN, Director.

THE SCHOOL OF FINE ARTS offers the best possible facilities for study in all departments of *Drawing, Oil* and *Water Color Painting, Architectural Modelling, Sculpture,* etc., under the most competent specialists.

IT IS THE AIM OF THE CONSERVATORY to offer an education in the *Fine Arts* as thorough and complete as is given in the best schools abroad.

THE MANY ADVANTAGES of the school include the convenient arrangement of the art rooms, finely lighted and ventilated studios, and a complete collection of casts from the antique; the finest reproductions of drawings from the best French and German masters; also a collection of paintings and still life objects. Models five days each week. The association with the kindred arts of *Music* and *Elocution* in this great *Conservatory* assures a *School of Art* unsurpassed in this country.

STUDENTS OF THE ART DEPARTMENT are admitted *free* to all the *Collateral Advantages* offered in the *Musical* and other departments of the institution, which consists of *Concerts, Lectures, Library, Gymnasium,* etc.

A SAFE AND INVITING HOME is provided for lady students in the Conservatory building.

For calendar and special art circular, address

FRANK W. HALE, Gen'l Manager,
Franklin Square, Boston, Mass.

The Principal Art Institutions and Clubs of the United States.

ALBANY, N. Y.

THE ALBANY ART LEAGUE. Social organization of those interested in art. No classes of instruction connected with the League.

STATE CAPITOL. Important as an architectural work. Contains the two pictures by the late Wm. Morris Hunt, "The Flight of Night," and the "Discoverer."

ALBUQUERQUE, NEW MEXICO.

NEW MEXICO EXPOSITION AND DRIVING PARK ASSOCIATION. Under the patronage of this Association are classes in painting, sculpture, drawing, etc., etc.

Exhibition of work in September.

AMHERST, MASS.

AMHERST COLLEGE. There is a gallery of art connected with the college. The curriculum embraces a course of lectures on the history of sculpture in the second year.

AUSTIN, TEX.

THE WOMAN'S EXCHANGE. Similar to the various decorative art societies.

BALTIMORE, MD.

BALTIMORE CHAPTER OF THE AMERICAN INSTITUTE OF ARCHITECTS. MARYLAND HISTORICAL SOCIETY. Athenæum Building. Organized in 1844. There is a very fine art gallery connected with the Society, open to the public daily.

MARYLAND INSTITUTE. Organized in 1848. The Institute maintains a School of Art and Design. The curriculum embraces a complete course of elementary artistic, industrial, mechanical, and architectural drawing.

Exhibitions of the students' work in June. Through the liberality of the late Geo. Peabody, the Institute offers prizes amounting to $500 to the highest graduate.

PEABODY INSTITUTE. Founded by the late Geo. Peabody. The gallery of art, opened in 1881, contains a very fine collection of casts from the antique and Renaissance period.

BERKELEY, CAL.

UNIVERSITY OF CALIFORNIA. Possesses the Bacon art gallery of the University of California. It had its origin in a gift from Henry D. Bacon, of Oakland, Cal.

BOSTON, MASS.

See " Boston Art Guide."

BLOOMINGTON, ILL.

HISTORICAL AND ART SOCIETY. No replies to inquiries.

BROOKLYN, N. Y.

THE ADELPHI ACADEMY. Lafayette Avenue, corner St. James Avenue. Incorporated in 1867. Contains in its curriculum a Department of Fine Arts under the direction of J. B. Whittaker. The regular course is four years, and is very complete.

BROOKLYN ART ASSOCIATION. 179 Montague Street. Instituted in 1861 ; incorporated in 1864. Maintains, in conjunction with the Brooklyn Institute, the Brooklyn Art School, where splendid facilities are offered for the study of art. There are regular exhibitions held by the Association of oils and water colors.

BROOKLYN ART CLUB. Organized 1879. Secretary, W. Wadsworth. Annual exhibition in February.

BROOKLYN INSTITUTE. Founded in 1824; incorporated in 1890. Among the several departments of the Institute are those of Fine Arts, Architecture, Photography, and Numismatics. The Institute also maintains a Summer School of Art at Shinnecock Hill, L. I., and the Brooklyn Architectural School.

THE PRATT INSTITUTE. Founded through the generosity of Charles Pratt, one of the largest institutions of the kind in the country. The course of instruction in the Art Department includes the Regular Art Course, the Normal Art Course, Clay Modelling, Architectural and Mechanical Drawing, Applied Design, Wood Carving, and Art Needlework.

LONG ISLAND HISTORICAL SOCIETY. Pierrepont Street, corner Clinton Place. Incorporated 1867. The Society possesses a museum of works of art, relics, and curiosities, which are of historic interest in the development of this country.

THE REMBRANDT CLUB. Organized 1880. Secretary, Walter K. Payne. 31 Schermerhorn Street. Is a social organization of those interested in art.

BUFFALO, N. Y.

BUFFALO FINE ARTS ACADEMY. Maintains a permanent gallery of art. There is an art school connected with the Academy.

THE BOHEMIAN SKETCH CLUB. J. Francis Brown, Secretary, address at the Academy. Is a fine organization of artists. Their first exhibition has just been held at the Academy.

CHARLESTON, S. C.

THE CAROLINA ART ASSOCIATION. Organized in 1857. Washington Square. Sustains a fine art school exhibition of students' work early in June.

CHICAGO, ILL.

ART INSTITUTE OF CHICAGO. 202 Michigan Avenue. Charles L. Hutchinson, President; N. H. Carpenter, Secretary; W. M. R. French, Director. Permanent exhibition. Art school in connection with the Institute.

THE COSMOPOLITAN ART CLUB. Charles F. Browne, Secretary. 249 Wabash Avenue. Annual exhibitions.

DECORATIVE ART SOCIETY. 34 and 36 Washington Street. Objects, to create in Chicago a desire for artistic decoration, and to provide training in artistic industries. Classes in pencil and crayon drawing, painting in oil and water colors, china decoration maintained by the Society. Loan exhibition held. Secretary, Mrs N. S. Davis, Jr.

THE PALETTE CLUB. Organization composed of women. Secretary, Miss Virginia A. Murphy. 2220 Prairie Avenue. Annual exhibitions held at the Art Institute Building in the fall.

THE CHICAGO SOCIETY OF ARTISTS. 26 Van Buren Street. President, C. E. Boutivoo; Secretary, W W. Vernon. One of the most important clubs in Chicago. Annual exhibition in May at the Art Institute Building. Oils and water colors.

CINCINNATI, O.

CINCINNATI CHAPTER OF THE AMERICAN ARCHITECTS.

CINCINNATI MUSEUM ASSOCIATION.

CINCINNATI ART CLUB. 24 West 4th Street. L. H. Meakin, Secretary. Two annual exhibitions, May and November.

THE ART ACADEMY OF CINCINNATI. Is maintained by the Association. Course includes drawing, painting in oil and water colors, sculpture, pen drawing, decorative design. The Academy also maintains a Summer School from July to Sept. 1

THE CINCINNATI POTTERY CLUB. Organized in 1879. Ladies only, number limited to fifteen.

COLUMBUS, O.

THE COLUMBUS ART ASSOCIATION. Organized 1879. Y. M. C. A. Building. Maintains an art school, which includes complete course in art. Annual exhibition of students' work in June. A special art exhibition of the Association will be held during Lent, 1893. John E. Hussey, Secretary.

DAYTON, O.

LADIES' ART ASSOCIATION. Maintains a school which furnishes instruction in drawing and painting.

AMATEUR SKETCH CLUB. Miss Yunckel, Secretary. Annual exhibition in November. Organized 1891.

DENVER, COL.

ACADEMY OF FINE ARTS ASSOCIATION. This is an art school, under the patronage of the Association.

DETROIT, MICH.

DETROIT MUSEUM OF ART. Maintains the Detroit Art School, instruction in drawing, designing, and architecture. A. H. Griffiths, Secretary.

ITHACA, N. Y.

CORNELL UNIVERSITY. Has a fine museum, in which are some valuable collections of medals, gems, and medallions, and a fine architectural library.

ITHACA BRANCH OF THE SOCIETY OF DECORATIVE ART, NEW YORK.

JACKSONVILLE, ILL.

ART ASSOCIATION. Annual exhibitions are held. Courses of lectures and instruction given at its meetings.

MADISON, WIS.

STATE HISTORICAL SOCIETY. State Capitol. The art gallery of the Society contains pictures, principally portraitt and a cabinet of antiquities, coins, and Revolutionary relics.

MILWAUKEE, WIS.

MILWAUKEE COLLEGE. For women only. Has a very fine Art Department, where exceptional facilities are offered for the study of art.

MILWAUKEE INDUSTRIAL EXPOSITION. Exposition Building. The Association holds annual expositions and therewith art exhibitions.

MILWAUKEE MUSEUM OF FINE ARTS. Maintains the School of Design.

NEW LONDON, CONN.

NEW LONDON COUNTY HISTORICAL SOCIETY. Museum of exhistorical relics, Indian curiosities, etc.

NEW ORLEANS, LA.

SOUTHERN ART UNION AND WOMAN'S INDUSTRIAL ASSOCIATION. Maintains a school of design, in which there are both day and evening classes. The Association also maintains a salesroom, where the works of contributors are sold on commission.

NEWPORT, R. I.

NEWPORT HISTORICAL SOCIETY. Collection of Indian relics and antiquities.

REDWOOD ATHENÆUM AND LIBRARY. Incorporated 1747. One of the oldest institutions of the country. It possesses a very fine art collection.

RHODE ISLAND CHAPTER OF THE AMERICAN INSTITUTE OF ARCHITECTS.

NEW YORK, N. Y.

AMERICAN INSTITUTE OF ARCHITECTS. 18 Broadway.

AMERICAN WATER COLOR SOCIETY. 51 West 10th Street. Secretary, C. H. Eaton. Has a residet membership of 74, and 22 non-resident members. The exhibitions of this club confined to water colors. The exhibitions of the New York Etching Club are held at the same time and place with the Water Color Society. These exhibitions are the most important of their kind in the country.

ARCHITECTURAL LEAGUE. American Art Society Building. Secretary, Edmund T. Hapgood. Objects of the society, the promotion of architecture and the allied fine arts. The membership list numbers 213.

ARTISTS' FUND SOCIETY. Organized 1859, incorporated 1861. Secretary, G. H. Jewell. Is an organization of professional artists for the purpose of giving aid to disabled members. The Society has three funds: (1) The Widows' Fund; (2) The Relief Fund; (3) The Benevolent Fund, for the benefit of artists who are not members of the Society.

ARTISTS' AID SOCIETY. 51 West 10th Street. Secretary, J. C. Nicholl. Organized 1890. It is composed of artists, associated for mutual assistance and benefit. Has a fund of over $1,000. Membership of 52.

AMERICAN FINE ART SOCIETY. Incorporated 1889. Formed by a combination of the Society of American Artists, the Architectural League, and the Art Students' League, for the purpose of erecting a Fine Arts Building. The building on 57th Street, between Broadway and 5th Avenue, is now owned by the Society.

THE ART STUDENTS' LEAGUE. 143 West 23d Street. Founded 1875; incorporated in 1878. Miss Ellen K. Leute, Secretary. Composed of artists and art students. There are 260 active members. A splendidly equipped art school is maintained by the League. Astor Library, founded and endowed by John Jacob Astor, has a very fine collection of works on archæology and architecture. There is also a small collection of paintings and bronzes loaned by the Astor family.

CENTURY ASSOCIATION. 7 West 43d Street. Founded in 1847; incorporated in 1857. Secretary, Henry Howland. Is one of the most important art clubs in New York. It possesses a very fine permanent collection. There are regular exhibitions held each month. Admission to the exhibitions obtained through invitation by the members.

CHAMBER OF COMMERCE. Mutual Life Building. Possesses a large collection of portraits, including some specimens of early American artists.

COOPER UNION. 7th Street, corner 4th Avenue. Founded by the late Peter Cooper. Secretary, Abram S. Hewett. The library contains 30,000 volumes. Maintains a free art school for women.

GENERAL SOCIETY OF MECHANICS AND TRADESMEN OF THE CITY OF NEW YORK. Mechanics' Hall, 18 East 16th Street. Chartered 1792. Is a very wealthy society; maintains a splendidly equipped library, and a free evening school of drawing. There are besides free scholarships in Columbia College and University of New York within the gift of the Society.

LADIES' ART ASSOCIATION. 23 East 14th Street. Incorporated 1877. Objects, to promote the interests of women artists, and to found a central point of union and reference for its members, to provide instruction for those already engaged as teachers of painting and drawing in schools and colleges.

METROPOLITAN MUSEUM OF ART. Central Park, 5th Avenue, and 82d Street. Chartered 1870. The trustees of the Museum have established one of the finest art schools in the country.

THE NATIONAL ACADEMY OF DESIGN. Corner 4th Avenue and West 23d Street. Incorporated 1828. Possesses a fine collection of foreign and American pictures, and a large collection of casts for the use of the schools. One of the best equipped art schools in the country is maintained by the Academy. Two exhibitions annually are held.

THE NEW YORK SCHOOL OF APPLIED DESIGN FOR WOMEN. 200 West 23d Street. Instruction given in all branches of industrial art.

NEW YORK SOCIETY OF KERAMIC ARTS. Organized 1892. Two exhibitions annually, November and February. Secretary, Mrs. E. C. Dean.

NEW YORK ETCHING CLUB. Secretary, Chas. T. W. Neitalz. Objects, to advance the art of freehand etching. Forty-two members. Exhibitions are held at the same time and place as the American Water Color Society.

NEW YORK HISTORICAL SOCIETY. 170 Second Avenue. Instituted in 1804. In addition to a magnificent library, the society possesses in its museum the celebrated Abbott collection of Egyptian antiquities.

NEW YORK INSTITUTE FOR ARTIST ARTISANS. 140 West 23d Street. Ex-Gov. Joshua L. Chamberlain, President. T. W. Stimson, Educational Superintendent of Industrial Art School.

SALMAGUNDI CLUB. 49 West 22d Street. Incorporated 1880. Secretary, R. C. Minor. Society of artists. Only object, the promotion of social intercourse among artists, and the advancement of art by means of frequent exhibitions. Number of members, 124.

SKETCH CLUB. 47 West 42d Street. Incorporated 1892. Secretary, J. N. Hutchins. Object, the study of architecture and the allied arts. Number of members, 105. The Club has two exhibitions. First, exhibition of sketches in October, and the annual exhibition in December.

SOCIETY OF AMERICAN ARTISTS. Founded 1878. Secretary, W. A. Coffin. Number of members, 135. Holds regular annual exhibitions. Fourteenth exhibition held at the 5th Avenue galleries from May 2 to May 8 inclusive.

THE SOCIETY OF DECORATIVE ART. 28 East 21st Street. Incorporated 1878. Provides a place for the exhibition and sale of art work, and maintains a school of instruction.

PHILADELPHIA, PA.

ACADEMY OF FINE ARTS. Founded in 1805. One of the important institutions of the country. Has a magnificent collection of works of art. Holds two regular exhibits annually: oils in November, and water colors in April. Connected with the Academy is a very fine art school. Milton Bancroft, Superintendent.

DREXAL INSTITUTE. Chestnut Street, corner 32d Street. Founded by Anthony T. Drexal. Was opened Dec. 17, 1891. The chief object is the extension and improvement of industrial education. The Art Department is one of the most important features.

FRANKLIN INSTITUTE. 7th Street. Founded in 1824 by Samuel V. Merrick. Connected with the Institute is a drawing school, the chief aim of which is to further industrial art.

HISTORICAL SOCIETY OF PHILADELPHIA. 22 Spruce Street. Founded in 1824. Collection of portraits, paintings, and engravings of historic interest.

INDEPENDENCE HALL AND NATIONAL MUSEUM. Old State House. Collection of portraits of the signers of the Declaration of Independence.

MUSEUM AND SCHOOL OF INDUSTRIAL ART. Memorial Hall, Fairmount Park. Incorporated 1876. Object, the establishment of an institution like the South Kensington Museum and school in London. The school furnishes such instruction as is required by designers and workmen in the various constructive and decorative arts.

PHILADELPHIA ART CLUB. 220 South Broad Street. Incorporated 1887. Secretary, L. M. Miller.

THE PHILADELPHIA SCHOOL OF DESIGN FOR WOMEN. Broad and Master Streets. Founded in 1844 by Mrs. Sarah Peter, and incorporated in 1853. Is the pioneer of all industrial art schools in the United States. Its objects are to give women an opportunity to gain thorough and systematic instruction in practical designing. Thorough courses in portrait and landscape painting. Pen and ink sketching for process reproduction etching, china painting, modelling, wood engraving, and flower painting are open to students, as well as a special course for those who wish to teach. Emily Sartaris is the principal.

PHILADELPHIA SKETCH CLUB. 11th, corner Walnut Street. Organized 1860, chartered 1889. Objects, social intercourse among artists, artistic practice. Exhibitions annually. Secretary C. F. Seise.

PITTSBURG, PA.

PITTSBURG SCHOOL OF DESIGN FOR WOMEN. Incorporated 1865. Exhibition of students' work in January.

AMATEUR ARTISTS' ASSOCIATION. At the Pittsburg School of Design.

PITTSBURG ART SOCIETY. 170 4th Avenue. Chas. W. Scoville, Secretary. In connection with this Society, there has been opened a permanent exhibition of pictures.

PLYMOUTH, MASS.

PILGRIM SOCIETY. Museum of relics, etc.

PORTLAND, ME.

PORTLAND SOCIETY OF ART. 507½ Congress Street. Special exhibition held annually. Walter Clifford, Secretary. 57 Exchange Street.

PROVIDENCE, R. I.

PROVIDENCE ART CLUB. 11 Thomas Street. Two exhibitions held annually.

RHODE ISLAND SCHOOL OF DESIGN. Furnishes instruction in drawing, painting, modelling, and designing. 283 Westminster Street.

QUINCY, ILL.

QUINCY ART ASSOCIATION. No replies to inquiries.

RICHMOND, VA.

RICHMOND ART ASSOCIATION. Organized 1878. 819 East Main Street. Annual exhibition in May. Maintains an art class.

VIRGINIA HISTORICAL SOCIETY. Chartered 1834. Westmoreland Club House. Possesses a fine collection of portraits, relics, etc.

ROCHESTER, N. Y.

POWERS ART GALLERY. Established by D. W. Powers, 1875. One of the most noted galleries of art in the United States.

ROCHESTER ART CLUB. Savings Bank Building. Organized in 1877. Annual exhibition in April. Art classes maintained by the club.

ROCHESTER ART EXCHANGE. 191-196 Powers Building. Organized 1880, for the exhibition and sale of art work. Free classes in charcoal drawing and embroidery sustained by the club.

SALEM, MASS.

ESSEX INSTITUTE. Incorporated 1848. Contains an art library and art collection. Course of lectures on art given during the winter season.

PEABODY ACADEMY OF SCIENCE.

SAN FRANCISCO, CAL.

SAN FRANCISCO ART ASSOCIATION. 430 Pine Street. Organized 1871. Maintains the California School of Design. Annual exhibitions are held.

SOCIETY OF DECORATIVE ART OF CALIFORNIA. 631 Sutter Street. Organized 1881. Maintains classes in drawing, painting, and art needlework. Annual exhibition in April.

ST. LOUIS, MO.

THE ST. LOUIS ARTISTS' GUILD. Miss M. Bruere, Secretary, 2670 Washington Avenue.

SCHOOL OF FINE ARTS. Art Department of Washington University, 19th Street and Lucas Place. Established 1879. Halsey C. Ives, Director. The University possesses a splendid permanent collection of works of art.

SOCIETY OF ARTISTS. Organized October, 1892. Only professional artists eligible to membership. Number of members, 26. W. A. Griffith, Secretary. Address, School of Fine Arts. Two annual exhibitions in November and April.

ST. LOUIS KUENSTLERVEREIN. Society of professional artists. Chiefly Germans. Have just dedicated one of the finest galleries in the West, at 1824 Chouteau Avenue. Emile Mench, Secretary.

SYRACUSE, N. Y.

SOCIAL ART CLUB. Organized 1875. Ladies only. Club possesses quite a valuable collection.

UTICA, N. Y.

UTICA ART ASSOCIATION.

WASHINGTON, D. C.

THE CORCORAN GALLERY OF ART. The gift of W. W. Corcoran.

WASHINGTON ART CLUB. Corcoran Building. An art school is maintained by the Club.

The Development of Art in Boston.

THE history of the art of painting in Boston, as told in its various collections, takes us back to the period about 1650. The specimens that have survived from this period would hardly be called "fine" to-day. Nevertheless, evidence exists which proves the fact that the art of painting in this city antedates that of any city in the country. The portrait of John Winthrop at Harvard must have been painted before 1649.

Very little is definitely known of Boston art until we come to Pelham and Smybert, who came to this country about 1726. Pelham was a portrait painter, a steel engraver, and land surveyor, but his chief title to fame rests in the fact that he was the step-father of Copley, and in all probability Copley's earliest efforts were the fruit of Pelham's teachings. Pelham painted portraits of Cotton Mather, Rev. Mather Byles, Dr. Timothy Cutler, president of Yale College, and many others; he made engravings of most of his paintings. Two of his engravings are in the Old South Church collection.

Smybert came from Scotland along with Dean Berkley; he painted portraits of many of the celebrities of that day. There is a portrait of Judge Edmund Quincy in the Museum of Fine Arts, and one of John Lovell in Harvard Memorial by Smybert.

Jonathan B. Blackburn, who came here in 1750, is the next portrait painter of any importance. There is a portrait by him of Col. Jonathan Warren in the Museum of Fine Arts. With Copley the true history of art in Boston begins. Prior to his leaving Boston in 1774, he is said to have painted over 300 portraits of the most famous people of that day. The now famous Copley Square was named after this artist. The Museum of Fine Arts contains several fine Copleys; among them are the famous portraits of John Hancock and Samuel Adams, but probably the best examples of his work are the Boylston portraits at Harvard College. There are several of his portraits in the Old State House. A fine example of his later work, painted in England, "Charles I. demanding in the House of Commons the Five Impeached Members," is the property of the Boston Public Library; it hangs in the Fine Arts Room, and was given to this institution by the Hon. Josiah Quincy and eleven other citizens. It is 90 x 121 inches. There are about sixty figures in the composition. All the heads are portraits from paintings by Vandyck and other contemporary artists. There is a portrait engraving by Copley in the Old South Church of the Rev. Wm. Wellsteed. Copley left Boston in 1774, and spent the rest of his life in England.

Col. John Trumbull, an officer in the Revolutionary Army under Washington, and a native of New Haven, forsook the sword for the brush while the Revolution was still in progress, and took Symbert's old studio on Tremont Row, between Brattle Street and Cornhill, for a short time. Here he painted pictures of John Hancock and other local heroes of the Revolution. He exhibited his picture of the Declaration of Independence, now in the Rotunda of the Capitol at Washington, in Faneuil Hall in 1818. Many examples of Trumbull's work are to be found in the Museum of Fine Arts, among them are: "The Sortie from Gibraltar," "Priam and the Dead Body of Hector," and portraits of Mr. and Mrs. Stephen Minot. In the Memorial Hall at Harvard College are some of his most important portraits, Washington, John Adams, and Christopher Gore, the latter a replica of the portrait in New Haven. His famous picture, the "Battle of Bunker Hill," is in the Yale gallery; Trumbull was adjutant of the first regiment of Connecticut, stationed at Roxbury on the day when the battle was fought.

Art in Boston received a fresh and important impetus in 1806 when Gilbert Stuart, a native of Rhode Island, arrived here, at the age of fifty, after having lived in London, Dublin, New York, Philadelphia, and Washington. He lived here the remaining twenty-two years of his life, and was buried in the cemetery on the Common. Stuart is looked upon to-day as perhaps the best portrait painter of his time; most of his pictures are in admirable condition, probably because he never blended his colors. While in England he had been associated with Sir Joshua Reynolds, Gainsborough, Sir Thomas Lawrence, Benjamin West, Sir Henry Raeburn, and others, and had opportunities to study the best examples of English art of that period. The Museum of Fine Arts contains some of the best examples of his work. Here are the famous Athenæum portraits of Washington and his wife, the "Washington at Dorchester Heights," the portraits of Gen. Knox and Josiah Quincy, also a slight sketch of himself. His first studio was in Washington Place, Fort Hill; he afterwards moved to Essex Street, near Edinboro Street.

Washington Allston, a native of South Carolina, came to Boston in 1818, when he was thirty-nine years of age, and lived mostly in Cambridge during the remaining twenty-five years of his life. He was the lion of Boston art in his day;

the friend of Longfellow, Lowell, Emerson, and the celebrities of his time; he was regarded as a sort of American Titian by his admirers. The critics of that period raved over his sentimental productions. His large unfinished picture of "Belshazzar's Feast" hangs in the Museum of Fine Arts, also his "Rosalie," "The Flight of Florimel," "Elijah Fed by the Ravens," "The Rising of a Thunder-Storm at Sea," the portrait of Benjamin West, of Isaac of York, and a portrait of himself. There are many of his tracings and unfinished paintings in the Museum also. Allston was much admired by his contemporaries, and he wielded a strong influence over such men as George Fuller, Henry Sargent, Chester Harding, D. C. Johnston (Boston's first caricaturist of note), Joseph Ames, Francis Alexander, T. Buchanan Read (the artist and author of "Sheridan's Ride"), R. M. Staigg, and many others. Most of these artists were members of the Boston Artists' Association of which Allston was the first president. Col. Henry Sargent painted the portrait of Peter Faneuil, which now hangs in Faneuil Hall. James Frothingham, born in 1786, was also much influenced by Allston; he painted the portrait of Samuel Dexter, which now hangs in the Harvard Memorial.

Samuel F. B. Morse, the famous inventor of telegraphy, was a pupil of Allston, with whom he went to London in 1811 for a short stay; while in London he studied with West and Copley; he was afterwards elected president of the National Academy of Design. The portrait of Noah Webster, engraved as a frontispiece to the dictionary, is from a drawing by Morse.

Chester Harding, born in 1792, was the rage in Boston about 1823. He painted the full-length portrait of Daniel Webster and Chief Justice Marshall, now in the Athenæum. Harding was a backwoodsman, and to a certain extent a self-taught man. He went to England and met with some success there, painting portraits of the poet Rogers, the historian Alison, and many others.

Alvan Fisher, born in 1792, flourished at this same period. Several examples of his work are in the Harvard Memorial Hall.

Gilbert Stuart Newton, born in 1792, a nephew and pupil of Stuart, painted genre subjects mostly. In the Museum of Fine Arts are several of his pictures, among them his "Forsaken," which somebody at the time called the painting of "a sob." The portraits of John Adams and Fisher Ames are after Stuart. There is a portrait of Samuel Appleton by him in the Harvard Memorial Hall.

Thomas Doughty, born the same year as Newton, was a native of Philadelphia, but moved to Boston. He was one of the most accomplished of early American landscapists. Doughty's small paintings are rare to-day. The British minister to the United States paid him twenty-five hundred dollars for one of his pictures.

Francis Alexander, born in 1800, a friend of Stuart's, was a successful portrait painter. He painted the portrait of Joseph Tuckerman in Harvard Memorial, and the portrait of Francis C. Gray in the Museum of Fine Arts.

G. P. A. Healy, born in 1808, was a celebrated portrait painter. He painted the portrait of Longfellow as a young man in the Museum of Fine Arts; here also may be found the portrait of himself as a young man. The work by which he is best known is the famous painting in Faneuil Hall of Webster replying to Hayne; it measures 16 x 30 feet, and contains about 130 figures, nearly all of which are accurate portraits. There is a full-length portrait of Mrs. Harrison Gray Otis, Jr., in the Old State House, by him.

Joseph Ames, born in 1816, was another "self-made" artist, and a friend of Allston's. He painted portraits of Lincoln, Webster, Choate, Prescott, Emerson, and Pius IX. His Lincoln and Choate are in Faneuil Hall. In the Museum of Fine Arts hangs his Webster, and in Harvard Memorial is his portrait of President Fulton. He also painted the famous "Death of Webster."

Richard M. Staigg was a miniaturist and *genre* painter. He painted some celebrated miniatures of Webster, Everett, and Washington Allston.

T. Buchanan Read, born in 1822, lived in Boston from 1842 to 1846. He was secretary of the Artists' Association. His poem, "Sheridan's Ride," made him famous. His painting of Longfellow's children in a group attained a great deal of popularity.

William Dunlap was a portrait painter. He exhibited in 1822 a large picture, "Christ Rejected," and painted several portraits here. He wrote a history of the "Rise and Progress of the Arts of Design in the United States," a good share of which was devoted to his own performances.

R. A. Salmon was an Englishman who lived on a rude wharf at South Boston, about this period, and painted marines.

Edward G. Malbone, the famous miniaturist, was a close friend of Allston's, he was a native of Newport. His stay in Boston was short. There is an excellent miniature of Mrs. James Carter in the Museum of Fine Arts by him. Malbone died in Charleston, S. C., at the age of thirty.

William Page, born in 1811, was one of the most famous portrait painters of his day — about 1845. The portrait of John Quincy Adams in the Museum of Fine Arts is a very fine piece of work. Many of his portraits are in the Harvard Memorial Hall. James Russell Lowell dedicated one of his volumes to Page. He was a very fine draughtsman.

About 1852, the most famous landscapist in Boston was Joseph Morvillier, a Frenchman. He painted certain phases of nature with a great deal of feeling.

Hammat Billings was regarded as the best illustrator in the country during the period about 1860.

With the advent of William Morris Hunt about 1861, came a new era in art. His influence still lives, as many of the prominent painters of to-day can testify. Fresh from the schools of France and Italy, burning with enthusiasm for the paintings of Millet and the Barbezon school, he became an influence immediately. His "Prodigal Son," "Girl at the Fountain," "Girl Reading," and study for the figure of Fortune, are hung at the Art Museum. Hunt exerted a marked influence on Ames, Johnston (the son of the caricaturist), Bicknell, Cole, Fisher, Fumen, Gay, Lafarge, Robinson (the famous cattle painter), Vedder, and many others who have since become famous, and specimens of whose work may be seen at the Art Museum.

Richard H. Fuller, the Chelsea watchman, became famous about this time for his delicate landscapes, one of which hangs in the Art Museum. Dr. Rimmer was at this time a unique figure in art in Boston, where his peculiar talents were best appreciated by the artists and students.

George Fuller, born in 1822, will ever remain one of the most unique personalities in American art. The Art Museum contains several of the finest examples of George Fuller's work, among them the famous "Arethusa."

This brief sketch merely outlines the history of painting in Boston up to a recent period.

Art Institutions and Collections.

THE BOSTON ATHENÆUM.

10½ BEACON STREET.

Officers.— President, Samuel Eliot; Vice-President, J. Elliot Cabot; Treasurer, Charles P. Bowditch; Secretary, William R. Richards; Trustees, Edward N. Perkins, Francis Parkman, George W. Wales, Arthur T. Lyman, John C. Gray, H. C. Lodge, Howard Stockton, Russell Gray, Roger Wolcott, Edward J. Lowell, George B. Shattuck, Thornton K. Lothrop, Charles C. Jackson, Barrett Wendell, T. W. Minns.

The Athenæum is a private association controlled entirely by shareholders. The library, however, which contains about 150,000 volumes very rich in work of art, is easily accessible to students who are not shareholders.

The first exhibition of paintings was held at its old quarters on Pearl Street, in 1826. There were annual exhibitions until 1849, at which date the institution was moved to its present quarters on Beacon Street.

For a long time the upper floor was devoted to an art gallery, the only kind of a permanent exhibition in Boston. In this gallery the collections of the present Museum of Fine Arts were exhibited, and on the completion of the Museum most of the art treasures were deposited with the new institution.

Of the pictures and sculpture which it retained, the casts of Ball Hughes's statue of Dr. Bowditch and of Houdon's Washington, Greenough's boy with eagle in bronze, and some casts from the antique, are placed in the vestibule. On the staircase are hung Leslie's portrait of Benjamin West, after Lawrence Harding's Daniel Webster, and Chief Justice Marshall. Cole's immense " Angel appearing to the Shepherds," Sully's portrait of Col. T. H. Perkins, Neagle's " Patrick Lyon at the Forge." A landscape by Allston, several copies from the old masters. Paintings by Allston, Stuart, Inman, Waldo, and Sully; and sculptures by Dexter, Gould, Powers, Crawford, Ball Hughes, Frazer, Greenough and Clevenger are in the reading-room and various other rooms.

The library is open from 9 A. M. until 6 P. M. The works of art in the vestibule and about the staircase are free for inspection. Permission to see the other rooms can be obtained from the librarian.

There are also a Claude, one Murillo, and two Guidos.

THE BOSTON MUSEUM OF FINE ARTS.
COPLEY SQUARE.

Was incorporated in 1870. Objects, to erect a museum for the preservation and exhibition of works of art, making, maintaining, and exhibiting collections of such works, and affording instruction in the fine arts. It is governed by a Board of Trustees, to include three appointed by Harvard College, three by the Boston Athenæum, and three by the Massachusetts Institure of Technology, and *ex-officio* the Mayor of the city, the President of the Trustees of the Public Library, and the Superintendent of the Public Schools, the Secretary of the Board of Education, and the Trustee of the Lowell Institute of Design. The income of the Museum is derived from subscriptions, legacies, and donations, from entrance fees, and from the interest on various endowment funds. The present building was erected from plans by Sturgis & Brigham, and is at present only one third of the size contemplated. The Museum, though perhaps not the richest, is one of the most systematic and complete collections in the country, and therefore invaluable educationally. In its collection of Egyptian antiquities, Assyrian, Greek, and Roman sculpture, it illustrates nearly every phase of the development and decline of ancient sculpture.

The minor arts of the ancients too are well illustrated by the very rich collection of bronzes, earthen and glass vessels, and a complete set of electrotypes of ancient coins published by the South Kensington Museum.

The collections of architectural casts are very rich. The sculpture of the Renaissance and its industrial arts and of mediæval Europe are well represented in ceramics, enamels, textiles, carvings, metal work, etc.

Of the Dutch school it contains some of the very best examples, including canvases by Rysdael, Teniers, Metzu, Cuyp, Netscher, Maas, Verelst, Van Hysmun, Kalf, and a small Rubens.

The English school is represented by Sir Peter Lely, of Charles II.'s time, Sir Joshua Reynolds, Gainsborough, Lawrence, Constable, William Etty, Robert Barrett Browning, son of the poet, and others. The Italian school is represented by a Sienese altar piece from the Renaissance period, with paintings by Bartolomeo Vivarine, a sketch of the Assumption by Tintoret, a "Christ and the Woman of Samaria" by Carlo Maratti, three paintings by Luca Giordano, two paintings by Giovanni Palo Pannini, and several others.

There are three pictures from the German school, Cranach's "Deposition from the Cross," a Holbein, and a landscape by Rosa di Tivoli.

The French school, from the seventeenth century to the present time, is very well represented; there are examples of Santerre, Chardin, Boucher, Greuze, Gericault, Ary Scheffer, Corot, Troyon, Courbet, Rousseau, Millet, Couture, Bastian Le Page, Dore, and Regnault. The "Quarry," by Courbet, was originally purchased by the Allston Club at the suggestion of Mr. A. H. Bicknell in the spring of 1866. The much-discussed "Joan of Arc," by Bastien Le Page, is among the examples of the later French school, also Regnault's "Automedon with the Horses of Achilles."

The room devoted to sculpture contains casts of some of the most celebrated Greek, Roman, and modern sculpture.

The Egyptian Room contains some very interesting specimens of mummies, sarcophagi, sculpture, coins, and interesting archæological and ethnological bric-a-brac.

The Japanese Department contains the great collection of pottery by Prof. Morse, and probably the finest collection of Japanese prints and painting in existence, belonging to Prof. Fenellosa. The Chinese Room contains some very fine examples of patient art work.

The Museum also contains some very rare engravings, both copper, steel, and wood, including examples of Durer, Rembrandt, Turner, and some choice proofs of the later French and English engravers.

A distinctive feature of this collection is the American Department. The interest shown by the institution in the etchings, engravings, etc., of this country has resulted in a very complete collection of this branch of art.

THE BOSTON MUSEUM.

The Boston Museum, opened at its present quarters, 28 Tremont Street, in 1847. It is the oldest existing theatre in Boston, and formerly was known as the Boston Museum and Gallery of Fine Arts, the exhibition of pictures, statuary and curios taking precedence to the stage performance. That order is quite reversed at present, but something of the old character is retained in the large hall, [which serves as a foyer to the theatre. In connection with the ordinary collection of pictures, casts, and curiosities are some good examples of American art: Rembrandt Peale's "Roman Daughter," painted 1820; "Gen. Washington and his family," painted by Savage (engraved by the painter himself); "The Signers of the Declaration of Independence," by the same artist; Charles Wilson Peale's portrait of David Rittenhouse; Winstantly's portrait of John

Adams; Pine's "Mad Woman in Chains"; Sully's "Passage of the Delaware." There are a few good old pictures by European artists.

HARVARD MEMORIAL HALL.
CAMBRIDGE.
CAMBRIDGE AND QUINCY STREETS.

The dining hall of this building, which was erected in commemoration of the students who fell in the service of their country, contains a large and valuable collection of portraits and portrait busts, mostly of persons connected with the college as officers or benefactors. The collection is very valuable and important as showing the development of portrait painting in the United States. There are, besides some old pictures of indifferent value, good examples of the following painters: Smybert, Copley (several, including the fine portrait of Mrs. Thos. Boylston Savage, portrait of Washington), Stuart, Sully, Frothingham, Trumbull, Newton, Alexander, Alvan Fisher, Bass Otis, Chester Harding, Page, Healy, Hunt, Hayward, Joseph Ames, and Cobb. There are busts by Houdon, Lander, Hiram Powers, R. S. Greenough, H. Greenough, Carew, Story, Crawford, Clevenger, and Dexter.

There is also a beautiful stained-glass window by La Farge in the building.

FANEUIL HALL.

Faneuil Hall, one of the chief historic buildings in Boston, contains the immense picture measuring 16 x 30 feet, "Webster replying to Hayne in the U. S. Senate, Jan. 26 and 27, 1830," painted by Geo. P. A. Healy. A key to the picture can be obtained of the superintendent for ten cents. Numerous portraits of celebrated Americans, especially those associated with the history of Massachusetts, hang upon the walls, and there are a few busts on the platform. The most notable among the old pictures, such as Copley's John Hancock and Samuel Adams, have been removed to the Old State House and Museum of Fine Arts, and replaced by copies. The hall is open daily from 10 A. M. to 5 P. M., from April 1 to Oct. 1, from 10 A. M. to 4 P. M. the rest of the year.

THE BOSTON PUBLIC LIBRARY.

At present located on Boylston Street, near Tremont, was founded in 1852.

The library contains a very complete list of books on art topics. In 1852 it was the recipient of $100,000 in money and books from Joshua Bates of London, after whom the upper hall was named. The famous Cardinal Tosti's collection of steel engravings, containing about 6,500 prints, was purchased by the late Mr. Thomas Appleton and given to the library. Many of these engravings are hung upon the walls, but most of them are in large portfolios in Bates Hall.

In the Fine Art Room is Copley's painting of "Charles I. demanding in the House of Commons the Five Impeached Members." There are works in marble in this room by Ball, Greenough, Story, Albertine, and Troschel. In the Trustees' Room are two portraits of Franklin, one by Greuze and the other by Duplessis. There are also portraits of Joshua Bates, by Eddis; Edward Everett, by J. Harvey Young; and Charles Sumner, by Moses Wright. Access to this room can be obtained by application at the desk in Bates Hall. A number of busts, etc., are scattered throughout the various rooms of the library.

THE MASSACHUSETTS HISTORICAL SOCIETY.
30 TREMONT STREET.

Was founded in 1791. The membership is limited to 100. The officers of the society are: president, George Edward Ellis; vice-presidents, Francis Parkman, Charles Francis Adams; recording secretary, Edward James Young; corresponding secretary, Justin Winsor; treasurer, Charles Card Smith; Librarian, Samuel Abbott Green; cabinet-keeper, Fitch Edward Oliver; members at large of the council, Edward Jackson Lowell, Edward Griffin Porter, Henry Fitch Jenks, Horace Elisha Scudder, Solomon Lincoln.

It contains, in addition to a very fine library, which can be used by any one introduced by a member, many valuable relics and some interesting portraits, among which are those of Governor Endicott Winslow (believed to be by Vandyke); Pownall, a copy by Henry C. Pratt; Dudley Belcher, Winthrop, Hutchinson, and Strong, by Chester Harding.

There is also a portrait of John Adams, by Gilbert Stuart Newton. A copy of a portrait of Sir Richard Saltonstall by Rembrandt. A copy of an excellent portrait of Sebastian Cabot from an original said to be by Holbein. Portraits by Stuart, of Allen, Edward Everett (unfinished), and Lieutenant-Governor Cobb, and others by Henly, Osgood, Sargent, Marston, and Wright.

THE OLD STATE HOUSE.

The exterior of the building, the old council chamber, and representatives' hall of the provincial period, have been restored as nearly as possible to their original form. There are, besides many valuable relics of early Massachusetts history, some interesting works of art. Copley's portraits of Samuel Adams and John Hancock are here. A Washington by Stuart, painted for Josiah Quincy in 1810 from an engraving and the artist's recollection. A very early picture by Moses Wright, "The Laying of the Corner-Stone of Beacon Hill Reservoir, Nov. 22, 1847," and a number of other old portraits and early views in and about Boston, all of which have an historic interest. The State House is open during the week from 9.30 A. M. until 5 P. M.

OLD SOUTH CHURCH.

WASHINGTON STREET, CORNER MILK.

There are many historical associations connected with this building, and they are enhanced by the museum of colonial, Revolutionary, and other relics collected within its walls. In the collection are some good specimens of the work of the early engravers, such as Pelham's portrait of Cotton Mather, engraved by him in 1727; John Adams, engraved by Geo. Graham; the Rev. William Wellstead, painted and engraved by Copley, 1753; Paul Revere, "Bloody Massacre," etc.

There are also some paintings, among them being a full-length of Edward Everett by Henry C. Pratt, a little known New England artist. Open from 9 A. M. until 6 P. M. Admission, twenty-five cents.

Art Clubs and Associations of Boston.

THE BOSTON ART CLUB.
Corner Dartmouth and Newbury Streets.

Is the most important of the art clubs in the city, and contains perhaps the best collection of recent local paintings. The club was organized in 1855, Joseph Ames being the first president. It was to a certain extent the outgrowth of the New England Art Union, which was organized three years previous to this date, and with the exception of the Boston Artists' Association, of which Allston was president, and the Allston Club, of which Hunt was president, it was the first serious attempt at an artists' organization in Boston. The club was incorporated in 1871, and in 1889 the club was authorized to hold real and personal property to the extent of $300,000. The success of the club financially and artistically has been most pronounced. It occupies a very beautiful club-house at the corner of Dartmouth and Newbury Streets, and is one of the most democratic and hospitable clubs in the city.

It has a fine library, a splendid gallery for exhibition purposes, and every equipment necessary to the existence of the modern club.

One feature of the club is an evening class under the instruction of Ernest Major. Two annual exhibitions are held: those for 1893, being, oils, Jan. 30 to Feb. 18; water colors, pastels, sculpture, etc., from April 7 to April 29. Admission to the club exhibitions are practically free, as tickets can be obtained from any member of the club. There is a membership of about 750. The officers are:—

President, Stephen M. Crosby; vice-presidents, Thomas Allen, Benjamin C. Clark; treasurer, Samuel N. Aldrich; secretary, Arthur D. McClellan; librarian, Samuel S. Curry; executive committee, elected in 1893, Nathanal J. Rust, Ross Turner, Charles H. Allen, John W. Leghton; elected in 1891, John J. Enneking, Albert L. Newman, Theodore H. Tyndale, N. Wilbur Jordan; elected in 1892, Charles T. Gallagher, Alphonso S. Covel, William G. Preston, Frank H. Tompkins.

A list of the artist members is appended:—

Albee, Byron
Allen, Francis R.
Allen, Thomas
Andrew, George T.
Bailey, R. M., Jr.
Barnard, E. H.
Bartholomew, W. N.
Benjamin, S. G. W.
Berry, Nathaniel L.
Bierstadt, Albert
Bixbee, William J.
Bogle, James
Bott, James
Boyden, Dwight F.
Brackett, S. Lawrence
Brackett, Walter M.
Brammar, Joseph
Bricher, Albert T.
Brown, Edwin Lee
Bryant, Wallace
Burdick, Horace R.
Butler, Philip A.
Cabot, Edward C.
Carter, Charles M.
Champney, Benjamin
Champney, J. Wells
Churchill, W. W., Jr.
Closson, William B.
Copeland, Charles
Cowles, Frank M.
Cross, Anson K.
Cross, Henry C.
Cummings, Charles A.
Dallin, Cyrus E.
Dana, Charles G.
Dana, William Jay
Danforth, C. Austin
Day, Henry
Dean, Walter L.
Draper, Francis
Dunsmore, John W.
Eksergian, Carnig
Enneking, John J.
Faxon, John Lyman
Fisher, William N.
Flagg, H. Peabody
Foster, John B.
Fraser, John A.
Gallison, Henry H.
Gay, William Allan
Gilbert, Robert William
Griggs, Samuel W.
Haberstroh, Albert
Hallett, Hendricks A.
Hahn, George R.
Halsall, William F.
Hamilton, E. W.
Hardwick, M. H.
Hassam, F. Childe
Hatfield, Joseph H.
Hayden, Charles H.
Hewes, Horace G.
Hill, Thomas
Hitchings, Henry
Hudson, Edmund J.
Inness, George
Inness, George, Jr.
Ireland, Harry C.
Irwin, Benoni
Jackson, William H.
Johnson, Marshall, Jr.
Key, John R.

Kimball, C. F.
Kinsley, Edgar L.
Kitson, Samuel
Lansil, Walter F.
Leavitt, Edward C.
Leighton, Scott
Longfellow, William P. P.
McDonald, Donald
Meneghelli, Enrico
Merrill, Frank T.
Miles, John C.
Miller, Leslie W.
Millet, Frank D.
Moore, Frederick H.
Monks, Henry G.
Myrick, Frank
Neflin, Paul
Niles, George E.
Niles, William J.
Noble, W. Clark
Norton, William E.
Notman, James
Ordway, Alfred
Parker, Charles S.
Partridge, William Ordway
Pettee, William
Phelps, W. P.
Pierce, Charles F.
Pope, Fred
Preston, William G.
Prichard, J. Ambrose
Richardson, Frank H.
Robinson, William S.
Roos, Peter
Rotch, Arthur
Rowe, J. Staples
Ryder, Henry Orne
Sanderson, Charles W.
Sandham, Henry
Santry, Daniel F.
Sawyer, Roswell D.
Scott, John W. A.
Shapleigh, Frank H.
Shute, Augustus B.
Slafter, Theodore S.
Smith, E. Boyd
Steele, Thomas Sedgwick
Storer, Charles
Strain, Daniel J.
Stuart, Frederick T.
Stuart, Ronald A.
Talbot, Henry S.
Taylor, G. Wood
Teel, George A.
Tilden, George T.
Tolman, Stacy
Tompkins, Frank H.
Triscott, S. P. Rolt
Tuckerman, S. Salisbury
Turner, Charles H.
Turner, Ross
Von Hosselin, George
Vonnoh, Robert W.
Wagner, Jacob
Walker, Charles A.
Ware, William R.
Way, C. Granville
Weeks, Edward L.
Wilcox, John A. J.
Williams, Frederick D.
Woodbury, Charles H.
Young, J. Harvey

THE BOSTON ARCHITECTURAL CLUB.
Tremont Place.

Was organized in 1889 for the purpose of the study of architecture and increase the knowledge and appreciation of art, to advance the interests of the profession, and to promote friendly intercourse among the members. In connection with the club are evening classes for the purpose of drawing from life, pen and ink and water color, and there is also a sketch class.

In conjunction with the Boston Society of Architecture, important architectural exhibitions are held, the last one occurring from Oct. 28 to Nov. 4, 1891, at the new Public Library Building.

C. H. Blackall, President, Music Hall Building.
Geo. F. Newton, Secretary, 919 Exchange Building.

MEMBERS.— Professionals.

Adden, Willard P.
Alden, Charles H.
Aldrich, Will S.
Allen, Francis R.
Andrews, R. D.
Atherton, Walker
Ball, H. B.
Ballantine, George A.
Barker, Edward J.
Barton, George F.
Bemis, John W.
Benton, E. R.
Bigelow, H. F.
Bixby, C. W.
Blackall, C. H.
Blake, H. L.
Blaney, Dwight
Boone, Allen F.
Bosworth, W. W.
Bowditch, A. H.
Brown, Samuel J.
Browne, H. W. C.
Bubier, A. C.
Busworth, George F.
Cabot, Edward C.
Cabot, F. Elliott
Cabot, W. R.
Cate, John W.
Chandler, F. W.
Chandler, Jos. E.
Chapman, J. H.
Chase, W. C.
Clark, Eugene L.
Clark, W. J.
Cobb, Albert W.
Codman, Ogden, Jr.
Coit, Robert
Cole, George Warren
Coolidge, Charles A.
Cooper, Frank Irving
Corner, J. M.
Cram, Ralph Adams
Crockett, G. W.
Crosby, C. F.
Dana, Edward Percy
Darrow, Alfred L.
Dean, G. R.
Dexter, George B.
Dow, R. N.

Drew, Stephen A.
Driver, James
Dudley, W. N.
Dunham, Charles B.
Eastman, Alfred C.
Eastman, C. A.
Elliott, Ernest H.
Everett, A. G.
Faxon, John L.
Ferguson, Frank W.
Fernald, George P.
Fisher, Gordon R.
Ford, Lyman A.
Fowler, J. Chandler
Fowler, J. Sumner
Fraser, John
Frazer, H. S.
Gay, Joseph B.
Gibbon, Robert W.
Goodrich, D. P.
Gray, Arthur F.
Hale, D. C.
Hale, Herbert D.
Haley, John J.
Hall, John W.
Harding, George C.
Hayward, H. C.
Higginson, Augustus B.
Hill, C. M.
Holt, H. C.
Hooker, Richard
Howard, John G.
Howe, Wallis E.
Hoyt, Edward H.
Hoyt, W. S. S.
Hurd, B. F.
Hutchins, Franklin H.
Jaques, Herbert
Jenks, Barton P.
Jones, L. H.
Kavanaugh, James F.
Kendall, Frank A.
Kerr, William G.
Kilham, Walter H.
Lane, J. A.
Lebon, Charles P.
Lee, J. S.
Little, Arthur
Little, Charles A.

Mack, John A.
Maginnis, Charles D.
Magenigah, Harold
Maher, E. E.
Mann, J. R.
Mauran, J. L.
McClare, C. Herbert
McFarland, Clarence F.
McKay, H. S.
McLean, Wm. H.
Mears, Henry A.
Metcalf, P. B.
Morgan, Henry H.
Mooney, Chas. S.
Morse, Junius H.
Newcomb, E. A. P.
Newton, George F.
Nichols, Geo. Leslie
Nichols, W. H.
Northend, W. W.
Northey, H. W.
Overmire, E. P.
Palmer, Clarence F.
Parker, Herman
Patch, Charles E.
Peabody R. S.
Pease, Austin W.
Peters, W. Y.
Pratt, H. T.
Preston, W. S.
Pollard, Albert A.
Porter, Geo. J.
Raymond, Chas. H.
Rice, A. W.
Rice, Walter E.
Richardson, W. C.
Ripley, H. G.
Rogers, Edward Little
Ryerson, Grant D.
Schrender, Otto P.

Schiller, F. A.
Sears, W. T.
Simon, L. A
Smith, Frank P.
Smith, Frank W.
Soderholtz, E. E.
Spencer, R. C., Jr.
Sprague, Arthur C.
Stephenson, H. M.
Stevens, Edward I.
Stone, George W.
Sturgis, R. C.
Sullivan, Matthew
Tallant, Hugh
Taylor, Bertrand
Tracey, P. A.
Trowbridge, Alex. Buel
Tucker, Frank W.
Tuckett, Chas. R.
Untersee, F. Jos
Vallance, Hugh
Van Straaten, Jacque
Wakefield, F. M.
Wales, G. C.
Walker, G. H.
Walker, W. L.
Walsh, T. F.
Warren, H. L.
Watson, R. A.
Wells, W. S.
Wentworth, P. F.
Wentworth, W. P.
Wheelright, Edmund M.
Wetherell, Geo. H.
Wilkinson, Henry W.
Wilson, E. I.
Winslow, W. F.
Wright, A. H.
Wolf, Wiltsi F.
Zeigler, E. L.

NON-PROFESSIONALS.

Bacon, Chas. J.
Bacon, Francis H.
Baird, John C.
Baker, C. M.
Bates, H. D.
Brazer, Geo. S
Brown, C. Dudley
Casson, Robert
Clifford, H. E.
Corthell, W. G.
Crook, Ervin F.
Curtis, Geo. De Vere
Cutter, A. B.
Damrell, Capt. John S.
Davenport, A. H.
Deane, E. Eldon
Doering, H. E.
Dunham, Horace C.
Evans, John
Flagg, Louis C.
Ford, Edwin

Gibbs, Henry P.
Gregg, D. A.
Grueby, Wm. H.
Guild, Irving T.
Habestroh, A.
Jackson, Robert W.
Jones, Harvey L.
Keats, Geo. W.
Kimball, L. E.
Kingsbury, E. R.
Kirchmyer, I.
Landerkin, Chas E.
Lincoln, Jas. G.
Mann, J. Harry
Muldoon, John F.
Munn, Herbert W.
Munsell, A. H.
Norris, Wm. C.
Pennell, Henry B.
Perkins, Geo. W.

THE BOSTON ART STUDENTS' ASSOCIATION.

Founded in 1879. Incorporated 1888. The object being to supplement the academic training of the School of Art connected with the Museum of Fine Arts, to assist its members in their artistic career, to cultivate a spirit of fraternity among art students, and to promote the interests of art in the city of Boston. The Association is composed mainly of the students of the Art School of the Museum of Fine Arts. The membership is divided into four classes: Active, Associate, Life, and Honorary. Only those, however, who are practising or studying art or are engaged in a profession allied to art are eligible for membership.

Under the patronage of the Association there are life classes held during the winter months, afternoon and evening. Classes in pen and ink for process reproduction, composition, and a portrait practice class. The classes in pen and ink are free to the members of the Association and to the students of the School of Fine Arts connected with the Museum. For the life classes and portrait practice class a small fee is charged the members.

All the classes, however, are open to students of art, and all information may be obtained from Thos. N. Codman, Secretary, South Lincoln, Mass.

Regular exhibitions are held by the Association. Following is a list of active members:

Abbott, F. M.,
  Wellesley Hills.
Abbott, Holker,
  Wellesley Hills.
Abbott, J. C., Jr.,
  9 Beacon St
Abbott, Miss Lucretia,
  11 Commonwealth Ave.
Adams, J. W.
Alford, Miss Martha,
  Kent St., Brookline.
Allen, Miss Rebecca S.,
  132 Marlboro St.
Atwood, Mrs. Eugene,
  99 Clarke Ave., Chelsea.
Babbitt, Miss G. G
Bailey, Miss Amy E.,
  3 Dudley Place.
Bailey, Miss M. A.,
  Hotel Pelham.
Balch, Miss A. L.,
  Jamaica Plain.
Ball, Miss A. W.,
  26 Newbury St.
Bardwell, Miss Flora,
  19 Inman St., Cambridge.
Bartol, Miss E. H.,
  17 Chestnut St.
Barton, Miss M. L.,
  Salem.
Baylor, Armisted
Beattie, Herbert W.
Behenna, Mrs. C. H.
Bicknell, H. W.
Bingham, Miss K.
Blair, G. H.
Blaisdell, Mrs. Chas.
Blake, Miss A. D.
Blanchard, Miss H. T.
Blaney, Dwight

Bliss, Miss Laura W.
Bolton, J. F., Jr.
Bowditch, Miss C.
Bowditch, Miss Charlotte
Bowditch, Miss Katharine
Bradlee, Miss Sarah
Bradley, Mrs. S. H.
Brainard, Mrs. F. W.
Braman, Miss L. A.
Brauner, Olaf M.
Brooks, Miss Mary M.
Brown, Miss E. B.
Brown, Miss E. D.
Bromwitch, Mrs. L. S
Browne, H. W. C.
Browne, G. D.
Brown, Miss M. M.
Buckingham, Miss E. L.
Burke, Miss K. E.
Burrage, Miss C. E.
Cabot, W. C., 2d
Capen, Miss Florence
Carey, Arthur Astor
Colson, Emil
Chamberlain, Mrs. G. M
Child, Miss E.
Choate Mrs. C. F.
Churchill, Miss A. H.
Clement, E. H.
Clement, Mrs. E. H
Cobb, Miss E. F.
Codman, Miss Alice
Codman, Miss S. W.
Codman, Thos. N.
Conant, Miss L. M.
Coolidge, Miss I.
Coolidge, J. T., Jr.
Cordner, Miss Caroline
Corne, W. F.
Cox, Mrs. Frank

Cram, R. A.
Crocker, Mrs. C. M.
Crocker, Miss Marion
Croft, Mrs. Arthur
Crozier, Miss A. M.
Cummings, Miss E. G.
Cunningham, Mr. M. F., Jr.
Curtis, Miss. E.
Curtis, Miss M. B.
Cushing, O. W.
Cutler, C. G.
Cyler, J. P.
Dabney, Miss E.
Danforth, Miss M.
Davis, Miss
Decamp, Mrs. J.
Decombe, Miss Emile.
Doe, Miss Catharine
Dow, Arthur M.
Earle, Miss M. W.
Eastman, Mrs. E. E.
Eaton, Miss C. S.
Edgerly, Mrs. Henry
Eldridge.
Elliot, Mrs. Amory
Ellis, Miss E. W.
Ellis, Miss Lucy
Emerson, E. W.
Emery, Miss G. H.
Emery, Miss M. S.
Endicott, 3d, Mrs. William
England, Miss F. P.
Farrar, Miss Addie M.
Fellner, Miss Lillian
Fellonosa, E. F.
Field, Mrs. H. T.
Fisher, Miss M. L.
Fisher, R. A.
Folsom, Miss K. E.
Fowler, Miss Emery
Frost, G. H.
Frothingham, T. G., Jr.
Gardner, Mrs. E. K.
Gardiner, Mrs. H. B.
George, V. L.
George, Miss B. E.
Gleason, Miss Elizabeth
Goldthwaite, Miss C.
Goodhue, B.
Goodhue, H.
Goodwin, Miss E. F.
Goodwin, Miss M. E.
Grant, Miss L. J.
Gray, Miss F.
Greeley, Miss Charlotte
Greene, Miss C. S.
Green, Miss M. A
Greene, Mrs. Lilian
Greenleaf, Miss May W.
Guild, I. T.
Guild, Miss K. E.
Habestroh, Albert C.
Hackett, J.
Hadaway, W. S.
Hale, Miss M.
Hall, W. J.
Hallowell, G. H.
Hallowell, Miss M.
Hapgood, T. B., Jr.
Harding, Miss Florence

Harris, Mrs. F. W.
Harris, Miss Rose
Hartwell, Miss O. G.
Hawkins, J. W
Haynes, Miss Flora E.
Hayward, Miss F.
Hazelton, Miss M. B.
Heath, Miss E.
Hill, Miss L. M.
Hills, Miss L.
Hinds, Miss H.
Holden, Miss M. H.
Hollingsworth, Mrs. Mark
Howe, Miss Lois L.
Howes, Miss Edith
Hudson, C. W
Jacobs, Miss M. C.
Jones, Miss L. A
Joslyn, Miss R. R.
Kaan, Miss Emma
Kakas, Miss Emma
Kelley, Miss Elizabeth
Kilburn, Warren I.
Kingsbury, E. I.
Knowles, Mrs. A. V.
Knowles, Miss E.
Kronberg, Mr. Louis
Lawrence, Miss H. L.
Lea, Miss F. T.
Leach, Mrs. J. L.
Le Brun, Mrs. J. M.
Lee, Miss Laura
Lettlehale, Miss Nellie
Logan, R. H.
Lombard, Miss E.
Longfellow, A. W., Jr.
Lord, Miss Josephine
Loud, J. Prince
Luques, Frank
Lyman, Miss B. M.
MacMahon, Mrs. W.
Macomber, Miss M. L.
Mathes, S. H.
Mawhinney, Miss M.
McKay, Miss H. E
Meredith, Mrs. C. A.
Merrill, Mrs. E. F.
Maynard, Miss F.
Metcalf, Miss Alice
Milliken, Miss G.
Mixter, Mrs. S. J.
Montague, Miss F. S.
Moore, Mrs. A. F.
Moore, Miss E. G.
Morse, Miss Kate
Morse, Miss M. S.
Morse, Mrs. E. R.
Moseley, Miss H. G.
Mundy, Mrs. A. J.
Murphy, Miss G. E.
Myrick, Miss C.
Newman, Miss Roma
Nichols, Miss R. S.
Nowell, Miss A. G.
Nowell, Miss M. G.
Norton, Miss S. M.
Oliver, Miss J. N.
Oliver, Miss S. E. C.
Osborne, Miss H. F.
Osgood, Miss L. L.

Page, Miss Edith
Parker, Miss B. M.
Parker, Mrs. W. L.
Peabody, J. E.
Peabody, Mrs. W. E.
Peck, Mrs. J. R.
Peralta, De, Mrs. S. B.
Perry, Mrs. A. P.
Pettes, Miss H. F.
Pierce, W. H.
Pitman, Miss S. L.
Plaisted, Miss Z. M.
Pope, Miss Edith
Potter, E. C.
Pratt, Mrs. C. M.
Pratt, M. A.
Putnam, Miss A. C.
Putnam, Mrs. H.
Radford, Miss H.
Raymond, Miss K. T.
Reed, Miss J.
Rice, H. W.
Richardson, Mrs. J. B.
Richardson, Miss C. H.
Richardson, Miss M. N.
Rogers, Miss A. P.
Ross, D. W.
Russ, Harry
Ryder, Miss J. G.
Ryther, Mrs. M. R.
Sacker, Miss A. M.
Saunders, Miss C. H.
Scroñ, A. H.
Scudder, Mrs. J.
Sears, Miss M. C.
Seavey, Mrs. G. S.
Shattuck, Miss C.
Sheldon, Miss F. B.
Simmons, E. F.
Slaiter, Theodore
Smith, A. G.
Smith, Mrs. C. C.
Smith, Miss. E. B.
Smith, J. L.
Smith, Miss S. F.
Smith, Miss Susan E.
Soper, Miss Mabel B.
Starbuck, Miss Florence
Stearns, Robert
Stevens. Miss J. N.
Storrs, Miss Anna F.
Stuart, Miss Mabel

Sturdivant, Miss Florence
Sturgis, F. S.
Sturgis, Miss M. R.
Sturgis, R. C.
Sullivan, Mrs. J. L.
Swain, Miss H. J.
Swan, Miss E. C.
Talbot, Miss E. A.
Tash, Mrs. M. J.
Taylor, E. V.
Terry, Miss Agnes S.
Thayer, Miss Grace
Thayer, Miss K. M.
Thayer, Mrs. G. H.
Thaxter, Mrs. S. G.
Thatcher, Miss C.
Tolman, Stacy
Torrey, Miss Frances
Treadwell, Mrs. E. B.
Turner, Ross
Tyson, Miss G.
Van Baalen Miss F.
Van Du Zee, Miss E.
Veazie, Miss A. L.
Wadleigh, H. R.
Wait, Miss Lizzie F.
Wales, Miss S. M. L.
Warren, H. B.
Warren, H. L.
Weld, Miss Edith
Wesselhœft, Miss
Wheaton, F. B.
White, Miss M. B.
Whiting, Mrs. C. B.
Whitney, Miss E. E.
Whitney, Miss Mabel
Whittier, Miss G. T.
Willar, Miss Eleanor
Willard, Miss T.
Williams, Miss E. W.
Williams, Miss M. E.
Wilsons, Miss A. L.
Winkly, Miss C. M.
Winlock, Miss M. P.
White, Miss Rose
Whitcomb, Miss May
Wood, W. H., Jr.
Woodbury, Mrs. C. H.
Worthley, Miss E. B.
Young, H.

THE BOSTON CAMERA CLUB.

Was organized in 1882 and became a club in 1886. It is an outgrowth of the interest awakened in amateur photography. It has splendidly equipped club rooms at 50 Bromfield Street, where it provides facilities for the practice and conducting experiments in photography by the members.

Lectures are delivered and illustrated by prominent amateurs and professionals.

Once in three years the club holds an exhibition at the rooms of the Boston Art Club, and exhibitions are held at regular intervals at its own club room, 50 Bromfield Street. The next exhibition occurs the first week in January.

The following are the officers and members of the club:
President, Henry N. Swett.
Secretary, Wilbur C. Brown.

ACTIVE MEMBERS.

Allen, Francis R.	220 Devonshire St.
Ames, Winthrop	North Easton, Mass.
Anable, Frederick S.	70 Kilby St.
Andrews, Edward R.	119 Beacon St.
Austin, Arthur S.	48 Congress St.
Babcock, Thomas J.	32 Hamilton St.
Bacon, Francis W.	1746 Cambridge St., Camb'ge
Bailey, Jason S.	Corey St., West Roxbury.
Belknap, H. W.	50 Beacon St.
Blackall, Clarence H.	18 Music Hall Building.
Blake, Francis	Auburndale.
Briggs, William Sumner	The Warren, Roxbury.
Brown, Wilbur Cutter	Naval Office, Custom House.
Bullock, Rufus A.	66 Mt. Vernon St.
Cabot, George E.	24 Marlborough St.
Chase, Walter G.	10 Central St.
Chenery, Cornelius	194 Boylston St.
Chickering, George H.	791 Tremont St.
Cockayne, E. O.	711 Tremont St.
Codman, James M.	Brookline.
Crocker, Edgar	247 Commonwealth Ave.
Crowell, Horace S	Hunnewell Ave., Newton.
Currier, Charles H.	50 Bromfield St.
Dana, W. T.	71 Kilby St.
Dizer, Mrs. S. C.	236 Commonwealth Ave
Dodge, C. F.	218 High St.
Dodge, W. W.	72 Sparks St., Camb'ge.
Dorr, G. W.	P. O. Box 1376.
Dresel, E. L.	328 Beacon St.
Drew, W.	98 Monroe St., Lynn.
Eames, O. A.	658 Washington St.
Eaton, G. H.	10 Mt. Washington Ave.
Eddy, G. H.	2 State St.
Elliott, C. L.	176 Tremont St.
Field, P. B.	Charity Bld'g, Chardon St.
Forbush, Mrs. Linda W.	36 Hancock St.
French, W. A.	319 Washington St.
Frizzell, J. A.	138 K St.
Fuller, E. A.	246 Marlboro St.
Gorrie, J. M.	5 Central Wharf.
Greene, J. T.	1107 Washington St.
Haskell, E. M.	New Orleans.
Heath, E. N.	172 High St.
Hollingsworth	36 Federal St.
Hollingsworth, Z. T.	44 Federal St.
Holman, J. C.	134 Richmond St.
Hooper, S. H.	17 Congress St.
Hubbard, C. W.	133 Essex St.
Kimball, B.	2 Newbury St.
Latimer, H. A.	12 Milford St.
Lee, John C.	Mountford, Brookline.
Lewis, David W.	Hyde Park.
Lewis, William B.	22 High St.
Little, J. L.	Brookline.
Loud, J. Prince	135 Mt. Vernon St.
Lowell, Percival	53 State St.
Manning, Francis H.	138 Federal St.
Mason, Dr A. Lawrence	265 Clarendon St.
Mason, John S.	196 Marlborough St
Means, C. J.	41 Lincoln St.
Means, James	190 Beacon St.
Minot, Laurence	39 Court St.
Morgan, George M.	36 Canal St.
Noyes, Edward I. K.	P. O. Box 2360.

Packard, Dr. Horace . . . 3.. Commonwealth Ave.
Parker, E. Francis . . . Jamaica Plain.
Parker, Herman . . . . 228 Commonwealth Ave.
Pearson, Horace B. . . . 414 Marlborough St.
Pierce, Mrs. H. W. . . .
Pond, Quincy . . . . . Auburndale.
Pope, Walter F. . . . . 626 Atlantic Ave.
Pratt, F. Alcott . . . . 3 Somerset St.
Preston, Wm. Gibbons . . 186 Devonshire St.
Reed, J. A. . . . . . . 41 Clive St., J. P.
Reed, Wm. Garrison . . 11 Kilby St.
Rhoades, Albert L. . . . 45 Oliver St.
Rice, Harry L. . . . . . 125 Summer St.
Rothwell, William H. . . 100 Arch St.
Russell, H. C. . . . . . Marlboro, Mass.
Saville, M. H. . . . . . Peabody Museum.
Sears, Mrs. C. F. . . . . 132 Beacon St.
Shaw, John O., Jr. . . . 27 State St.
Sherman, William H. . . P. O. Box 2658.
Shillaber, Charles P. . . . 339 Beacon St.
Smith, Joseph N. . . . . 84 State St.
Snell, George . . . . . 110 Tremont St.
Sprague, Charles . . . . 380 Marlborough St.
Stackpole, Dr. Fred'k D. . 50 Dudley St., Roxbury.
Starbird, N. W. . . . . . 50 Bromfield St.
Stevens, Dr. Wm. Stanford 51 Devonshire St.
Stone, Frederick . . . . 407 Beacon St.
Storer, Charles . . . . . 25 Bromfield St.
Sweet, Henry N. . . . . 84 State St.
Tarbell, Dr. George G. . . 274 Marlborough St.
Thurston, John H. . . . 50 Bromfield St.
Treadwell, T. R. . . . . 63 Federal St.
Underwood, W. Lyman. . 52 Fulton St.
Webster, Augustus F. . . 55 High St.
Weeks, Nelson L. . . . . 67 Federal St.
Wells, James A. . . . . 2 Pemberton Sq.
Whiton, Morris F. . . . Hingham.
Wigglesworth, George . . 10 Marlborough St.
Wilmarth, Arthur R. . . 51 Elliot St., J. P.
Witherell, William O. . . 15 Warren Place, Roxbury.

ASSOCIATE MEMBERS.

Barrows, Fletcher L. . . . P.O. Box 44, Middleborough.
Dunham, Horace C. . . . Plymouth.
Eddy, Miss Sarah J. . . . Providence, R. I.
Lomb, Adolph . . . . . Rochester, N. Y.
Weeks, George W. . . . Clinton.
Wilson, Howell F. . . . Ballardvale.

HONORARY MEMBERS.

Chase, J. Eastman . . . 7 Hamilton Pl.
Crow, Prof. C. R. . . . . Institute of Technology.
Rowell, Frank . . . . . 485 Tremont St.

THE BOSTON SOCIETY OF WATER COLOR ARTISTS.

Formed some seven or eight years ago but lately reorganized. Is composed of some of the most prominent Boston artists, only men being eligible for membership. The purpose of the club is to hold exhibitions.

Their last exhibit was held at Chase's Gallery and closed Dec. 23. There will be annual exhibits of water colors. The following are the officers and members of the club:

President, Thomas Allen; Vice-President, Ross Turner; Secretary and Treasurer, Charles Copeland, 49 Studio Building.

MEMBERS OF THE CLUB.

Allen, Thomas	12 Commonwealth Av.
Boit, E. D.	
Barse, Geo. R.	
Caliga, I. H.	175 Tremont St.
Clements, G. H.	
Copeland, Chas.	40 Studio Building.
Dean, Walter L.	3 Pemberton Sq.
Fraser, John A.	114 West 18th St., N. Y.
Garrett, E. H.	Winchester.
Hallett, H. A.	42 Court St.
Hardwick, M. H.	12 West St.
Hassam, Childe	95 5th Ave., New York.
Little, Philip	Salem.
Peirce, H. W.	Revere.
Pierce, Chas. F.	12 West St.
Prichard, J. Ambrose	Evans House, 175 Tremont St.
Rotch, Arthur	85 Devonshire St.
Sandham, Hy.	152 Boylston St.
Stuart, Frederick T.	42 Court St.
Sargent, J. S.	
Smith, J. Linden	The Ludlow, St. James Ave., cor. Clarendon St.
Taylor, W. L.	Wellesley, Mass.
Triscott, S. P. R.	433 Washington St.
Turner, Ross	Salem.
Bixbee, W. J.	22 School St
Wagner, Jacob	22 Irvington St.

THE BOSTON WATER COLOR CLUB.

Was organized in 1887 for the purpose of holding an annual exhibition in water colors. It was formed about the same time as the Boston Society of Water Color Artists, but only women artists are eligible for membership. The sixth exhibition was held in December and the seventh exhibit will be held early in December of 1893. Mrs. Elizabeth F. Parker, 339 Marlboro' Street, is the secretary of the club. The following is a list of the artist members:

Mrs. Susan H. Bradley, Philadelphia.
Miss Mary K. Longfellow, Portland.
Miss Laura C. Hills, Newburyport.
Mrs. Helen B. Merriman, Worcester.
Mrs. Sarah W. Whitman.
Mrs. Emily D. Tyson.
Mrs. Eleanor W. Motley.
Mrs. Louisa Mason.
Mrs. Sarah C. Sears.

Mrs. Mary McG. Dalton.
Mrs. Marcia Oaks Woodbury.
Miss Silsbee.
Miss K. W. Lane.
Miss Mary M. Morse.
Miss Helen M. Hinds.
Miss Susan M. L. Wales.
Miss Annie C. Nowell.
Miss Frances B. Townsend.
Miss Alice M. Curtis.
Mrs. Elizabeth F. Parker, Secretary.

THE MINERAL ART LEAGUE.
2 PARK SQUARE.

This club was organized in 1892. It has for its object the study and advancement of china painting. The meetings are held the third Saturday of each month and are educational as well as social. The membership is confined to residents of Massachusetts, and is limited to one hundred and fifty. Applicants for admission to the club can have their names presented by any member. Exhibitions and sales will be held annually. The following is a list of the present members and their addresses:

Mrs. Marcus Beebe,
  Malden.
Mrs. H. A. Crosby,
  Eldredge St., Newton.
Miss K. R. Moulton,
  88 Boylston St.
Mrs. C. L. Swift,
  2 Park Sq.
Mrs. C. Bennett,
  131 Tremont St.
Miss Julia Perrin,
  2 Park Sq.
Miss Ella Fairbanks,
  15 Wellington St.
Miss E. P. Carter,
  68 W. Rutland Sq.
Miss E. E. Page,
  2 Park Sq.
Mrs. M. L. Warren,
  205 W. Chester Pk.
Mrs. Geo. Morse,
  Newtonville.
Mrs. Geo. Bateman,
  662 Shawmut Ave.
Mrs. M. W. Howard,
  3 Winter St.
Miss Edith Miles,
  232 School St.,
  Somerville.
Miss Grace Marsh,
  West Newton.
Miss Onata North,
  Prospect Hill,
  Somerville.
Mrs. Gertrude Davis,
  41 Essex St.
Miss A. J. Johnson,
  36 Upton St.
Mrs. Arthur Carroll,
  West Newton.
Miss J. N. Oliver,
  Lynn.
Miss Carrie F. Allen,
  136 W. Concord St.
Miss Abbie Rogers,
  Weymouth Centre.
Mrs. Lawrence Neebe,
  Winthrop Highlands.
Miss Ella Donkin,
  Newton.
Miss Clara Foster,
  Waltham.
Mrs. E. Hollis,
  62 Boylston St.

THE UNITY ART CLUB.
16 ARLINGTON STREET.

Was formed in 1889. Incorporated in 1891. Is an organization of artists and those interested in art, both men and women being eligible for membership. The club occupies very pleasant rooms on Arlington Street, and holds two exhibitions yearly; water colors early in December, and oils in the last part of February.

Under the patronage of the club is maintained a life class and evening drawing classes. Lectures and discussions on art topics form an important feature of the club meetings. Another important feature in connection with the policy of the club is the leasing during the summer months a cottage easily accessible to Boston which is at the disposal of its members. There are about one hundred and twenty-five members. The following are the board of officers and artist members:

President, Walter Gilman Page; Vice-President, Mrs. H. W. Chapin; Treasurer, Mrs. M. M. Everett; Clerk, Mrs. L. P. Thomson; Assistant Clerk, Mrs. I. H. Paige, and twelve Directors.

MEMBERS.

Badlam, Mrs. C. C.
Baker, Mrs. Katharine
Bailey, Mrs. E. H.
Barry, Miss A. J.
Bennett, Mrs. C.
Blanchard, Mrs. M. C.
Bowden, Mrs. S. S.
Boyle, Mrs. N. P.

Bunker, Mrs. C.
Barton, Miss May
Carpenter, Miss E. M.
Cowdery, Mrs. E. D.
Cowdery, C. H.
Cox, Miss F. E.
Crosby, Mrs. H. A.
Curtis, Mrs. M. B.
Durggin, Miss H. T.
Fairchild, Mrs. F. M.
Geer, Miss G. W.
Gorrie, J. M.
Greenwood, J. H.
Hathaway, Mrs. S. W.
Hollis, Mrs. E.
Jackson, W. H.
Jeffers, Mrs. H. M.
Johnson, Miss A. R.
Klumpke, Miss A. E.
Leavitt, Miss Agnes
Lewin, Mrs. L. F.
Macomber, Mrs. F. D.

McIntire, Miss Kate
Merrill, Miss A. W
Merritt, Miss Louisa
Monhon, Miss K. R.
Norwell, Miss Georgia
Norwell, Miss L. G.
Palmer, Miss Adelaide
Parsons, Miss C. L.
Page, Walter G.
Rice, H. W.
Ruggles, Mrs. T. A.
Sandham, Henry
Sanderson, Chas. W.
Swift, Mrs. C. L.
Swain, Miss H. J.
Staples, Miss A. K.
Taralta de, Mme. S.
Turner, C. H.
Tirrell, Miss Florence
Thompkins, F. H.
Watkins, Miss Kate
Whittemore, Mrs. F. B.

THE ST. BOTOLPH CLUB.

NEWBURY STREET.

Organized in 1880. Although not strictly an art club, has a decided artistic tendency, as its object is the promotion of social intercourse among artists and authors and others connected with or interested in art and literature.

The exhibitions of the St. Botolph Club are among the best known in Boston, and are very successful. There are two regular exhibits each year, one of water color and one of oils. These regular exhibits are supplemented by special ones at irregular intervals during the year. During 1892 ten exhibits were held. The following are the artist members of the club:

Allen, Thomas
Atwood, F. G.
Apoloni, Adolfo
Bartlett, N. S.
Brown, J. A.
Carlsen, Emil
Coolidge, J. T., Jr.
Ellwell, J. D.
Gaugengigl, I. M.

Gray, S. S.
Ibsen, L. S.
Langerfeldt, T. O.
Muncey, Geo. C.
Richardson, F. H.
Snell, Geo.
Vinton, F. P.
Williams, F. H.

THE PAINT AND CLAY CLUB.

419 WASHINGTON STREET.

Was organized in 1880. This club is rather a social although strictly an art association of the Bohemian Order and numbers among its members many prominent artists.

Its objects are the production of works of art, literature, and music. Some very unique exhibitions are held by the club.

The officers are: Thomas Allen, Chairman; J. M. Stone, Secretary, 23 Irvington Street; J. P. Rinn, Treasurer.

Following are the artist members:

Allen, Thomas . . . . . 12 Commonwealth Ave.
Andrew, Geo. T. . . . . 5 Temple Pl.
Atwood, F. G. . . . . 100 Chestnut St.
Bicknell, W. H. W. . . . Winchester.

Carlson, Emil
Caliga, J. H. . . . . . . 174 Tremont St.
Dean, Walter L. . . . . . 2 Pemberton Sq.
Downes, W. H. . . . . . Boston Transcript.
Enniking, J. J. . . . . . 174 Tremont St.
Graves, Abbott . . . . . 160 Boylston St.
Garrett, E. H. . . . . . Winchester.
Halsall, W. F. . . . . . 174 Tremont St.
Ordway, Alfred . . . . Studio Building.
Rinn, J. P. . . . . . . 104 Washington St.
Stone, J. M. . . . . . . 23 Irvington St.
Strain, D. J. . . . . . . 278 Boylston St.

ABSENT MEMBERS.

Barre, Geo. R., Jr. . . . Kansas City.
Clements, G. H. . . . . Tunis.
Davis, C. H. . . . . . . At Doll & Richards.
Edwards, Geo. W. . . . Plainfield, N. J.
Harran, F. C. . . . . . New York.
Smith, F. B. . . . . . . Paris.
Tuckerman, S. S. . . . . London.

The Art Stores of Boston.

Next to the Museum of Fine Arts, and the regular permanent institutions, the art interest of Boston is centred in the art stores. The heads of these various establishments are men of the keenest artistic taste, and sustain a well-deserved reputation for sound judgment in all art matters; and upon art interests of the city they exert a marked influence. Each of the more important art stores possesses a gallery, and in these galleries some of the most interesting and important exhibitions in the city are held; and the very finest examples of contemporary art, both American and foreign, are often found exhibited upon their walls. The changes in their galleries are frequent, and exhibitions and sales of the works of the well-known artists are being held at different intervals during the year, and the art lover is as familiar with the interior of the galleries of the art stores as with those of the regular art institutions. The most important of the art stores are: Williams & Everett, 130 Boylston Street, facing the Public Garden; Doll & Richards, 2 Park Street; J. Eastman Chase, 7 Hamilton Place; Walter Kimball & Co., 9 Park Street, and the E. W. Noyes Co., Bromfield Street. Under the head of exhibitions in Boston will be found, as far as practicable, the dates of the special exhibitions of these firms.

THE SOULE PHOTOGRAPH CO., 338 Washington Street. Has one of the largest collection of photographs on art subjects to be found in the United States.

# WALTER KIMBALL & CO.,

No. 9 PARK STREET.

IMPORTERS AND DEALERS IN

Works of Art.

𝔉ine 𝔓roof 𝔈tchings,
𝔈ngravings, 𝔚ater 𝔈olors,
𝔓hotographs, etc.

FRAMING OF ALL KINDS.
NOVELTIES IN LEATHER FRAMES, VIGNETTE, CARD,
AND CABINET SIZES.

Art Exhibitions for 1893.

THE ART MUSEUM. Copley Square. Permanent exhibition with two change exhibitions each year. Admission to the gallery twenty-five cents during the week. Free Sundays.

THE BOSTON ART CLUB. Two regular exhibitions. Oils from Jan. 19 to Feb. 18, inclusive. Water colors, pastels, sculpture, etc., from April 7 until April 29. Cards obtained from the members of the club admit visitors to the gallery.

BOSTON ART STUDENTS' ASSOCIATION. Regular exhibition of students' work from May 16 to May 28.

BOSTON CAMERA CLUB. Exhibitions of photographic work at the club room from Jan. 2 to Jan. 9.

THE BOSTON SOCIETY OF WATER COLOR ARTISTS. One regular exhibition each year of water color early in December. Gallery and exact date not definitely decided.

THE BOSTON WATER COLOR CLUB. Exhibition of water colors once each year.

COWLES ART SCHOOL. 145 Dartmouth St. Regular exhibition of work done by the students.

THE MASSACHUSETTS INSTITUTE OF TECHNOLOGY. Has a regular exhibit in the spring of the work done in the third and fourth year, by the students in the architectural department.

THE MASSACHUSETTS NORMAL ART SCHOOL. Regular exhibition of the students' work in June.

THE MINERAL ART LEAGUE. Exhibition and sale at 2 Park Square. Easter week.

THE PAINT AND CLAY CLUB. 419 Washington St. One regular exhibition during the year. This is a very unique exhibit, partaking of the nature of a burlesque.

THE SCHOOL OF DRAWING AND PAINTING. Museum of Fine Arts. Copley Square. Regular exhibition of students' work from May 10 to May 28.

ST. BOTOLPH CLUB. Two regular exhibitions annually, one of oils and one of water colors. These regular exhibitions supplemented by special exhibitions held during the year. Dates for 1893 not yet arranged.

THE UNITY CLUB. 16 Arlington St. Two regular exhibitions; oils early in February, and water colors early in December.

WILLIAMS & EVERETT. 190 Boylston St. Exhibitions continuous during the winter. A special exhibit of the works of some noted foreign artists will be held during January. This to be followed by the works of Miss Devereaux (a pupil of Duprez), in February.

DOLL & RICHARDS' GALLERY. 2 Park St. A permanent exhibition, also important special exhibits. Opening Jan. 13, and continuing two weeks, there will be a joint exhibition of the works of Miss Elizabeth B. Green and Miss A. E. Wadsworth.

J. EASTMAN CHASE'S. 7 Hamilton Pl. Will offer some important exhibitions by well-known foreign artists. The dates and names of the exhibitions not definitely arranged.

WALTER KIMBALL & CO. 9 Park St. A continuous exhibition of works of art at their gallery, supplemented by frequent special exhibits.

The Art Educational Institutions in Boston.

ALPHABETICALLY ARRANGED.

BOSTON TRAINING SCHOOL OF MUSIC.
MUSIC HALL BUILDING.

Organized in 1891. Has an art department under the able instruction of Henry Sandham, R. C. A., supported by an efficient corps of instructors. It is the aim of the school to give instruction in all branches of art, but especial attention is given to training in illustration.

THE BOYLSTON ART STUDIOS,
62 BOYLSTON STREET.

Mrs. E. Hollis, principal, is an art school especially designed for women. There is an able corps of instructors attached to the school, and all branches of art are taught.

The regular course includes: oils and water colors, landscapes, flowers, fruit, still life, and outdoor sketching.

Drawing connected with this department is a preparatory course for pupils who intend entering the Normal Art School.

Tapestries, and very complete department in china decoration.

THE CONSERVATORY OF MUSIC.
FRANKLIN SQUARE.

The Department of Fine Arts in this institution aims to give an education as thorough and complete as any in the country. It is especially intended to make this a training school for teachers as well as provide the best advantages for those who wish to make a study of the fine arts.

The course of study is of three years' duration, and is grouped into three divisions: Drawing and Painting, Modelling, and Decorative Design. The Board of Instructors includes: W. A. T. Claus, principal; Grace L. Temple, Frank Myrick, Cyrus Cobb, Edith Pope, Wm. J. Kaula. The many advantages of the school include a convenient arrangement of the art rooms, finely lighted and ventilated studios, a splendid collection of casts from the antique, and reproduction of drawings from the best French and German masters.

COWLES ART SCHOOL.

Established in 1873 by Frank M. Cowles. The school has one of the finest corps of instructors of any school in the city, including such names as: Ernest L. Major, Joseph Decaney, Henry H. Kitson, Bertram C. Goodhue, Mercy A. Bailey, Theo. A. Ruggles, Annie E. Riddell.

All departments of drawing (including cast and life) and painting are taught, including life class from the nude model, portraiture, antique, still-life, water color, modelling, illustrating, composition, and perspective. There is also an afternoon sketch class from model in costume, particularly interesting to illustrators.

The plan of the school has been, from its inception, to promote the advancement of art in America, a subject which engages the serious attention of artists, and all those interested in the progress of art in this country.

In addition to giving a continuous and thorough training in art, the school meets, in a wholesome way, the needs of a considerable number of earnest students who are not able to attend for long periods at a time, or who have been obliged to gain their instruction in an irregular and unequal way, and need to have their deficiencies made up in special lines of study.

The school is so arranged that, without detriment to the regular course, those who are not able to devote the entire season to the work can receive a month's instruction at a time, paying only for such instruction as they receive. It is the plan of the management to give to every pupil careful individual instruction.

In this way those who have studied hitherto desultorily and without instruction can have their faults quickly and permanently remedied. This individualizing of instruction in the school has been marked with most satisfactory results.

Another admirable arrangement is that by which professional artists can enter the school to work from the life model without instruction. In past years many have availed themselves of this privilege who had found it inconvenient to have the life model in their studios.

Each student, on joining the school, will be allowed to enter at once upon the highest grade of work of which he is capable, and he will be carefully advised and guided in his subsequent work. It is designed to establish a training school for those who wish to become professional artists, as well as for others who are interested in art.

The school points with pride to the success of its students who have gone abroad to continue their art studies, and those who have entered into the various avocations in the field of art.

All information in regard to the school may be obtained from Frank M. Cowles, 145 Dartmouth Street, Boston.

THE LOWELL SCHOOL OF PRACTICAL DESIGN.
Foot of Garrison Street.

Was established in 1872 by the Trustees of the Lowell Institute, for the purpose of promoting industrial art in the United States. The responsibility of conducting the school is borne by the Massachusetts Institute of Technology. The school is free to all pupils. The course of study is of three years' duration, and is essentially practical, there being a weaving room fitted with chain, gingham, and Jacquard looms attached to the school.

The course includes (1) Technical manipulation; (2) Copying and variation of designs; (3) Original designs or composition of patterns; (4) The making of working drawings and furnishing of designs.

The school is under the personal direction of Mr. Chas. Kastner, assisted in the weaving department by Louis W. Clark, and in the designing department by Mrs. Ella L. Shaw. For all information concerning the school apply to the Secretary of the Institute of Technology.

THE MASSACHUSETTS INSTITUTE OF TECHNOLOGY.
Architectural Department.

The course in architecture is designed to secure for its graduates a liberal education, as well as thorough professional training. It prepares them not only for their work as subordinates, when rapidity, skill, and taste in drawing and design will be most useful qualifications, but also for their subsequent independent career, when technical knowledge will become most important.

The Institute has this year completed a new building for this department, fully equipped with every material appliance required for the fullest and best professional and technical training.

The regular course is four years, and includes sketching and water color, freehand drawing, modelling, pen and ink sketching and drawing from life. The instructors in the architectural department are:

Francis W. Chandler, Professor of Architecture, in charge of the department; Eugene Létang, Professor of Architectural Design; Eleazer B. Homer, S. B., Assistant Professor of Architecture; William H. Lawrence, S. B., Instructor in Architecture; Robert S. Shedd, Assistant in Architecture; Ross Turner, Instructor in Sketching and Water Color; C. Howard Walker, Instructor in the History of Ornament; Charles L. Adams, Instructor in Freehand Drawing; Fred Law Olmsted, Lecturer on Landscape Architecture; Truman H. Bartlett, Lecturer on Modelling; D. A. Gregg, Instructor in Pen and Ink Sketching; Ernest L. Major, in charge of the Life Class. Annual exhibitions of the work done in the third and fourth years are held.

THE MASSACHUSETTS NORMAL ART SCHOOL.
Corner of Newbury and Exeter Streets.

Was established in 1873 as the result of an act of the Massachusetts Legislature of 1870, which made instruction in drawing obligatory in the public day schools, and required cities and towns containing more than 10,000 inhabitants to provide free instruction in industrial drawing to pupils over fifteen years of age. The school is intended to be a training school for teachers of industrial art, the specific aim at present being to prepare teacher instructors to teach and superintend industrial drawing in the public schools of the State. It also aims to provide for high skill in technical drawing, and for industrial art culture. The school offers a four-year course in the scientific and artistic branches and their practical application to industry, and a two-year course of training for the work of training and supervising drawing in the public schools. All students who wish to take either course are obliged to complete course A, a most complete course in elementary drawing. They are then free to exercise their choice in either the two-year course, which entitles them to a diploma certifying that they are fitted to teach or supervise drawing in the public schools, or the four-year course, which prepares them to teach the subject of industrial art.

The two-year class consists of Class A, Elementary Drawing, and Class C, Constructive Art and Design. The four-year course of classes A and B, Painting and Design for surface decoration; C and D, Modelling and Design in the round.

Tuition is free to residents in Massachusetts intending to teach.

To pupils outside the State, tuition is $50 per term.

The instructors are Geo. H. Bartlett, Principal; Albert H. Munsell, Mercy A. Baily, Anson K. Cross, M. Louise Field, George Tyson, Henry H. Kendall, Annie E. Blake, Edward W. D. Hamilton, John L. Frisbie.

THE SCHOOL OF DRAWING AND PAINTING OF THE MUSEUM OF FINE ARTS.

Founded in 1876. Ranks among the finest art schools in the United States.

The school is under a permanent committee, and to this committee the Trustees of the Museum of Fine Arts have granted, under certain conditions, the use of the museum, and the galleries are open to the students, Saturdays excepted, during the entire year. The regular course of the school is three years, and the courses of instruction embraced are: drawing from the cast; painting from the head, the draped model and still life, and drawing and painting from the nude model.

There is a very complete course in decorative design, including line drawing and the use of color. By arrangement with the Art Students' Association, pen and ink work for process reproduction and composition are taught. There will also be added this year a course in modelling.

A splendid course of lectures will be given on artistic anatomy, perspective (practical and theoretical), and Greek art.

There are six free scholarships within the gift of the school to pupils who have studied to the extent of six months, and through the generosity of the patrons of the school several prizes are offered for excellence in the pupils' work.

The instructors of the school are: Edmund C. Tarbell, Frank W. Benson, G. Howard Walker, J. L. Smith, E. W. Emerson, Anson K. Ross, Miss Elizabeth Child, and Miss A. P. Fitch.

A list of the students is appended :

Mr. J. W. Adams.
Mr. C. A. Aiken.
Miss R. G. Allen.
Mr. H. B. Ames.
Miss G. G. Babbitt.
Miss B. M. Bentley.
Mr. C. H. Blake.
Mrs. E. B. Blackford.
Miss E. Bowditch.
Miss K. P. Bowditch.
Miss E. Brown.
Miss M. M. Browne.
Miss G. M. Bryant.
Miss E. O. Bumstead.
Miss M. T. Cabot.
Miss F. J. Capen.
Miss G. L. Carpenter.
Miss A. H. Churchill.
Miss R. L. Clough.
Miss E. F. Cobb.
Miss A. N. Codman.
Mr. T. N. Codman.
Mr. E. F. Comins.
Miss R. L. Cousens.
Miss M. M. Crafts.
Miss L. P. Currier.
Miss M. H. Curtis.
Miss F. C. Cushman.
Mr. C. G. Cutler.
Miss M. L. Danforth.
Miss B. G. Davidson.
Miss D. M. Dill.
Miss C. Doe.
Miss E. Dorr.
Miss S. H. Duff.
Miss E. G. Elliott.
Miss I. B. Fellner.
Miss M. L. Fisher
Miss T. L. Forster.
Miss E. Fowler.
Miss J. B. Gammell.
Miss M. Gay.
Miss B. L. George.
Mr. F. W. Glover.
Mr. A. L. Gobeille.
Miss Belle Greene.
Miss M. A. Greene.
Miss E. Guerrier.
Mr. W. J. Gurry.

Mr. G. H. Hallowell.
Miss L. M. Hamill.
Miss A. Hapgood.
Miss F. W. Harris.
Mr. W. H. Haskell.
Miss E. R. Hawkes.
Miss M. B. Hazelton.
Mr. C. H. Hedge.
Mr. F. Hittl.
Miss M. B. Hobart.
Miss A. M. Hodges.
Miss L. Houghton.
Miss E. Howard.
Mr. V. Howes.
Miss C. M. Hudson.
Mr. C. W. Hudson.
Miss K. T. Ives.
Miss L. W. Jackson.
Miss K. A. Kimball.
Miss E. McL. King.
Miss E. Knowles.
Miss A. W. Ladd.
Miss C. F. Lamb.
Mr. H. T. Langmaid.
Miss F. T. Lea.
Miss A. F Lewis.
Miss M. A. Lincoln.
Miss S. E. Linnell.
Mr. R. H. Logan.
Mr. Wm. C. Loring.
Mr. J. E. McAllister.
Miss P. McKay.
Miss G. Milliken.
Miss F. S. Montague.
Miss E. G. Moore.
Mr. G. A. Morrison.
Mrs. F. B. Mundy.
Miss B. Mülle.
Miss A. Munyon.
Miss C. H. Myrick.
Miss R. S. Nichols.
Miss L. M. Norris.
Miss A. P. Osgood.
Miss E. Page.
Miss M. S. Peirce.
Miss C. G. Perry.
Miss E. S. Perry.
Mr. H. W. Perry.
Miss E. Pope.

Miss L. B. Putnam.
Miss R. Reynolds.
Miss E. Reynolds.
Mr. E. E. Riley.
Miss E. M. Roberts.
Mr. A. F. Schmitt.
Miss C. A. Shattuck.
Miss I. A. Shrimpson.
Miss E. B. Smith.
Miss E. H. Smith.
Miss C. F. Soule.
Miss B. M. Stanley.
Mr. R. C. Steadman.
Miss M. Stetson.
Miss A. E. Storrs
Mr. C. S. Strauss.
Miss G. Sturtevant.
Mr. R. Tappan.
Miss L. V. Taylor.
Miss C. Thacher.
Miss F. Torrey.

Mr. R. J. Tucker.
Mr. W. H. Upham.
Mr. G. A. Viles.
Mr. H. Vobis.
Miss L. G. Wadsworth
Mr. F. A. Webster.
Miss M. F. Wesselhoeft
Miss E. Whitaker.
Miss M. Whitcomb.
Mr. H. D. White.
Miss L. E. Whitman.
Miss A. L. Whitmore.
Miss E. C. Whitney.
Miss M. B. Whitney.
Miss M. S. Wood.
Miss. A. W. Woodbury.
Miss A. R. Warren.
Miss H. I. Stebbins.
Miss M. G. Nowell.
Miss M. S. Morse.

DECORATION CLASS.

Mr. F. J. Alford.
Miss A. P. Allyn.
Miss C. L. Bailey.
Miss A. L. Balch.
Mr. C. B. Bigelow, Jr.
Mr. P. H. Brigham.
Miss B. E. Coleman.
Miss A. E. Colvin.
Miss J. M. Conant.
Miss M. W. Conary.
Mr. C. N. Dennett, Jr.
Mr. W. A. Dickey.
Mr. W. M. Eddy.
Miss M. Eltz.
Miss G. H. Emery.
Miss E. I. Ewer.
Miss L. C. Felton.
Miss C. E. Folsom.
Miss L. A. Foster.
Miss G. C. Fuller.
Mr W. H. Garrett.
Miss A. Goodale.
Miss M. E. Goodwin.

Mr. W. S. Hadaway.
Mr. T. B. Hapgood, Jr.
Miss M. L. Hitchcock.
Miss M. H. Holden.
Miss E. L. Hull.
Miss A. D. Lovering.
Miss M. R. Mawhinney.
Miss M. C. Monks.
Miss A. J. Morse.
Miss G. E. Murphy.
Miss A. C. O'Brien.
Miss F. E. Potter.
Mr. M. A. Pratt.
Miss A. M. Sacker.
Miss A. I. Stevens.
Miss L. B. Stevens.
Miss M. B. Stevenson.
Mr. S. E. F. Spycee.
Miss M. C. Ware.
Miss A. C. Tilden.
Miss A. M. Tuttle.
Mr. W. H. Wood, Jr.
Mrs. Helen Richard.

BOSTON ARCHITECTURAL CLUB.
5 TREMONT PLACE.

Also maintains for the benefit of its members an evening life class, classes in water color and pen and ink. There is also connected with the club a sketch class.

THE UNITY ART CLUB.
16 ARLINGTON STREET.

Maintains a life class and classes in drawing.

THE YOUNG MEN'S CHRISTIAN ASSOCIATION.
BERKELEY, CORNER BOYLSTON STREETS.

Has an evening drawing class, under the instruction of Rudolph Guenthe.

THE YOUNG MEN'S CHRISTIAN UNION.
58 BOYLSTON STREET.

Also has evening drawing classes.

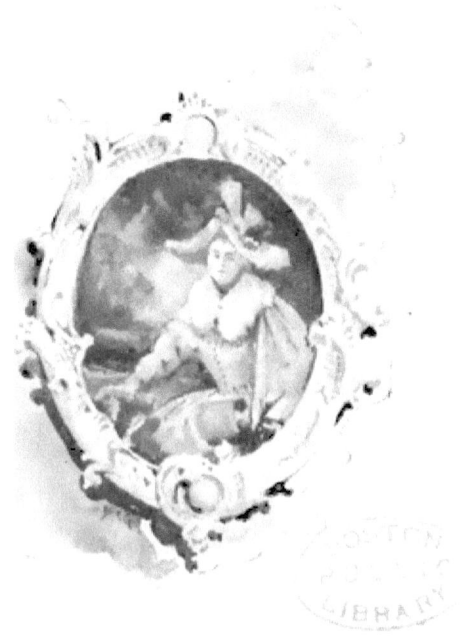

BOSTON ILLUSTRATING COMPANY,
7 State Street,
Boston.

Designing, Photo-Engraving,
Copper Half-Tones a Specialty.

THE BOSTON ART CLUB.
DARTMOUTH, CORNER NEWBURY.

Maintains an evening life class, under the instruction of Ernest L. Major, and evening drawing classes.

THE ART STUDENTS' ASSOCIATION

Sustains a life class, a practice portrait class, and classes in pen and ink for process reproduction. The last-named course is free to the members of the Association. All classes, however, are open to those not members of the Association. For information, address Thos. L. Codman, Secretary, South Lincoln, Mass.

Art Scholarships.

THE LONGFELLOW SCHOLARSHIP.

THERE are two art scholarships awarded in Boston, examinations for which are held at the Art Museum. One established by William Ernest Longfellow in 1888 is for men under thirty years of age, residents of New England, who are students of painting, dependent for support on their own exertions, and who propose to make painting a profession. The examination, which takes place in one of the rooms of the Art Museum, includes drawing the figure from the nude, sketching a composition in color, and painting a head from life. The scholarship entitles the winner to six hundred dollars per year for three years. The successful competitor is expected to pass three years among the art schools of Europe, the choice to be left to him with certain restrictions. He will be under the supervision of one or more American painters at the place where he may elect to go, and will be liable to have his stipend stopped at any time if the committee find that he is neglecting his work. If, on the other hand, the committee are of the opinion that he has done exceptionally well, he will receive at the end of his course a bonus of from fifty to one hundred dollars according to circumstances. He will be obliged to submit to the committee of the school results of his work.

CHANDLER PARIS PRIZE.

This prize consists of $900 a year, for the support of an art student in the study of drawing, painting, and decoration in Paris, for five years. If, however, after two years' work in Paris, the student should wish to work elsewhere, he may do so, if the jury consider him sufficiently advanced. The prize is subject to the following conditions:—

The prize is only open to those students who really need its financial aid to carry on their art studies abroad. The holder of the Paris prize will be expected to pursue some studies in the history of art, in connection with his main work. The competition is open to any man or woman over twenty-one years of age, resident in or coming from Massachusetts, or who has studied art in Massachusetts for the school year preceding the examination. By "coming from the State of Massachusetts" is meant a person abroad, whether carrying on art studies or otherwise, whose residence when in America is in Massachusetts.

No competitor shall have received a medal or honorable mention in any foreign art exhibition or salon.

Before receiving any money, the candidate is required to agree to send home, at the end of each year, specimens of his or her work, signed by the master under whom he or she has worked. If the work falls below the standard required by the jury, the jury shall, after assuring themselves that it is not merely a temporary fluctuation in the student's work, warn him or her that, unless the work reaches the required standard during the following year, the money will then be withdrawn and a new election held.

At the end of five years the student will be required to return to Boston and teach gratuitously twice a week for two years a class to be selected by the jury, the latter having discretionary power to modify this to meet any exigency that may arise in connection with the student's inability to sustain himself by the sale of his pictures. Such modification might permit him to admit students into his class who will pay for the instruction received.

The following French artists have signified their willingness to serve as a commission of control over the students sent by the Paris Prize to Paris: Messrs. J. L. Gerome, Puvis de Chavannes, Carolus Duran, L. Bonnat, P. A. J. Dagnan Bouveret, and Benjamin Constant. This commission will meet twice a year for a general examination of the work of the students, and will report upon it to the jury in Boston.

In Boston, the jury consists of the President of the Museum of Fine Arts, the Professor of the History of Art in Harvard University, the President of the St. Botolph Club, the President of the Boston Art Club, the President of the Boston Art Students' Association, and two artists chosen by the Boston Art Students' Association, and two artists chosen by the President of the Museum of Fine Arts.

James B. Potter, of Lawrence, pupil of Joseph De Camp, is the present holder of the scholarship.

THE ROTCH SCHOLARSHIP FOR ARCHITECTS.

The Rotch Scholarship for Architects was established by the children of B. S. Rotch, Oct. 1, 1883. It consists of $2,000 for two years, and enables the student to study and travel abroad during that time. The conditions are that the applicants shall be under thirty years of age, and shall have worked in an architect's office for two years. Competitions are held under the supervision of a committee of the Society of American Architects in the basement of the Museum of Fine Arts, Copley Square. The successful candidates so far have been A. H. Blackall, S. W. Meade, G. F. Newton, E. A. Joslin, A. W. Ford, H. H. Bacon, W. T. Partridge, and the prize is now held by R. C. Spencer. Further information may be obtained of H. Langford Warren, 9 Park Street, Boston.

In addition to the above scholarships, both the Cowles Art School and the Museum of Fine Arts School offer inducements to students in the shape of scholarships which enables the successful students to study without paying tuition for stated periods.

MISS DOROTHY DENE.

Reproduction from Photograph by Lux Engraving Co.'s Halftone
DUPLICATES FOR SALE.

LUX ENGRAVING CO.,
295 Congress St., BOSTON, MASS.

Halftone Process a Specialty. Catalogue, Book and
Magazine Illustrations Executed
Carefully and Promptly.

The Art Tariff
AND
The Law of Copyright,

COMPILED AND ARRANGED BY

EDWARD H. SAVARY, Esq.,

OF THE SUFFOLK BAR.

ACT OF OCT. 1, 1890.

An Act to Reduce the Revenues and Equalize Duties on Imports and for other Purposes.

Be it enacted by the Senate and House of Representatives of the United States of America in Congress assembled, that on and after the sixth day of October, 1890, unless otherwise specially provided for in this act, there shall be levied, collected, and paid upon all articles imported from foreign countries and mentioned in the schedules and paragraphs respectively prescribed, namely:

SCHEDULE A.

30. Ink and ink powders, printers' ink, and all other ink not specially provided for in this act, thirty *per centum ad valorem*.

50. Blues, such as Berlin, Prussian, Chinese, and all others containing ferrocyanide of iron, dry or ground in or mixed with oil, six cents per pound; in pulp or mixed with water, six cents per pound on the material contained therein when dry.

54. Ochre and ochrey earths, sienna and sienna earths, umber and umber earths, not specially provided for in this act, dry, one fourth of one cent per pound; ground in oil one and one half cents per pound.

56. Varnishes, including so-called gold size or Japan, thirty-five *per centum ad valorem*; and in spirit varnishes for the alcohol contained therein one dollar and thirty-two cents per gallon additional.

60. Zinc, oxide of, and white paint containing zinc, but not containing lead, dry, one and one fourth cents per pound; ground in oil, one and three fourths cents per pound.

61. All other paints and colors, whether dry or mixed or ground in water or oil, including lakes, crayons, smalts, and frostings, not specially provided for in this act, and artists' colors of all kinds in tubes or otherwise, twenty-five *per centum ad valorem*: all paints and colors, mixed or ground with water or solutions other than oil, and commercially known as artists' water-color paints, thirty *per centum ad valorem*.

97. Plaster of paris or gypsum ground, one dollar per ton; calcined, one dollar and seventy-five cents per ton.

100. China, porcelain, parian, bisque, earthen, stone, and crockery ware, including plaques, ornaments, toys, charms, vases, and statuettes, painted, tinted, stained, enamelled, printed, gilded, or otherwise decorated or ornamented in any manner, sixty *per centum ad valorem*; if plain white and not ornamented or decorated in any manner, fifty-five *per centum ad valorem*.

101. All other china, porcelain, parian, bisque, earthen, stone, and crockery ware, and manufactures of the same, by whatsoever designation or name known in the trade, including lava tips for burners, not specially provided for in this act, if ornamented or decorated in any manner, sixty *per centum ad valorem*; if not ornamented or decorated, fifty-five *per centum ad valorem*.

105. Flint and lime, pressed glassware, not cut, engraved, painted, etched, decorated, colored, printed, stained, silvered, or gilded, sixty *per centum ad valorem*.

106. All articles of glass, cut, engraved, painted, colored, printed, stained, decorated, silvered, or gilded, not including plate glass, silvered, or looking-glass plates, sixty *per centum ad valorem*.

111. All cut, engraved, painted, or otherwise ornamented or decorated glass bottles, decanters, or other vessels of glass, shall, if filled, pay duty in addition to any duty chargeable on the contents as if not filled, unless specially provided for in this act.

123. Marble of all kinds in block, rough, or squared, sixty-five cents per cubic foot.

124. Veined marble, sawed, dressed, or otherwise, including marble slabs and marble paving tiles, one dollar and ten cents per cubic foot (but in measurement no slab shall be computed at less than one inch in thickness).

125. Manufactures of marble not specially provided for in this act, fifty *per centum ad valorem*.

Schedule C.

130. Slates, slate chimney-pieces, mantels, slabs for tables, and all other manufactures of slate, not specially provided for in this act, thirty *per centum ad valorem*.

180. Steel plates engraved, stereotype plates, electrotype plates, and plates of other materials, engraved or lithographed for printing, twenty-five *per centum ad valorem*.

SCHEDULE M.

417. Printing paper unsized suitable only for books and newspapers, fifteen *per centum ad valorem*.

418. Printing paper sized or glued, suitable only for books and newspapers, twenty *per centum ad valorem*.

419. Papers known commercially as copying paper, filtering paper, silver paper, and all tissue paper, white or colored, made up in copying books, reams, or in any other form, eight cents per pound, and in addition thereto fifteen *per centum ad valorem*; albumenized or sensitized paper thirty-five *per centum ad valorem*.

420. Papers known commercially as surface coated papers and manufactures thereof, cardboards, lithographic prints from either stone or zinc, bound or unbound (except illustrations when forming part of a periodical, newspaper, or in printed books accompanying the same), and all articles produced either in whole or in part by lithographic process, and photograph, autograph, and scrap albums, wholly or partially manufactured, thirty-five *per centum ad valorem*.

422. Paper hangings and paper for screens or fireboards, writing paper, drawing paper, and all other paper not specially provided for in this act, twenty-five *per centum ad valorem*.

423. Books, including blank books of all kinds, pamphlets, and engravings, bound or unbound photographs, etchings, maps, charts, and all printed matter not specially provided for in this act, twenty-five *per centum ad valorem*.

SCHEDULE N.

459. Manufacturers of alabaster, amber, coral, . . . or of which these substances on either of them is the component material of chief value, not specially provided for in this act, twenty-five *per centum ad valorem*. . . .

465. Paintings, in oil or water colors, and statuary, not otherwise provided for in this act, fifteen *per centum ad valorem*; but the term "statuary" as herein used shall be understood to include only such statuary as is cut, carved, or otherwise wrought by hand from a solid block or mass of marble, stone, or alabaster, or from metal, and as is the professional production of a statuary or sculptor only.

FREE LIST.

On and after the sixth day of October, eighteen hundred and ninety, unless otherwise specially provided for in this act, the following articles when imported shall be exempt from duty:

491. Art educational stops composed of glass and metal and valued at not more than six cents per gross.

512. Books, engravings, photographs, bound or unbound etchings, maps and charts which shall have been printed and bound or manufactured more than twenty years at the date of importation.

513. Books and pamphlets printed exclusively in languages other than English; also books and music in raised print, used exclusively by the blind.

514. Books, engravings, photographs, etchings, bound or unbound, maps and charts imported by authority or for the use of the United States or for the use of the Library of Congress.

515. Books, maps, lithographic prints, and charts specially imported, not more than two copies in any one invoice, in good faith for the use of any society incorporated or established for educational, philosophical, literary, or religious purposes, or for the encouragement of the fine arts, or for the use or by order of any college, academy, school, or seminary of learning in the United States subject to such regulations as the Secretary of Treasury shall prescribe.

516. Books or libraries, or parts of libraries and other household effects of persons or families from foreign countries, if actually used abroad by them not less than one year, and not intended for any other person or persons nor for sale.

680. Plaster of paris and sulphate of lime unground.

692. Regalia and gems, statues, statuary and specimens of sculpture where specially imported in good faith for the use of any society incorporated or established solely for educational, philosophical, literary, or religious purposes, or for the encouragement of fine arts, or for the use or by order of any college, academy, school, seminary of learning, or public library in the United States: but the term "regalia" as herein used shall be held to embrace only such insignia of rank or office, or emblems as may be worn upon the person or borne in the hand during public exercises of the society or institution, and shall not include articles of furniture or fixtures, or of regular wearing apparel nor personal property of individuals.

757. Works of art, the production of American artists residing temporarily abroad, or other works of art, including pictorial paintings on glass imported expressly for presentation to a national institution, or to any State or municipal corporation, or incorporated religious society, college, or other public institution, except stained or painted window glass, or stained or painted glass windows, but such exemption shall be subject to such regulations as the Secretary of the Treasury may prescribe.

758. Works of art, drawings, engravings, photographic pictures, and philosophical and scientific apparatus brought by professional artists, lecturers, or scientists arriving from abroad for use by them temporarily for exhibition and in illustration,

HALF-TONE ENGRAVING ON COPPER FROM PHOTOGRAPH

FRANKLIN ENGRAVING CO.

Designers and Illustrators,

Office, 28 School Street,   Works, 65 Essex Street,

BOSTON, MASS.

promotion and encouragement of art, science, or industry in the United States, and not for sale, and photographic pictures, paintings, and statuary imported for exhibition by any association established in good faith and duly authorized under the laws of the United States or of any State expressly and solely for the promotion and encouragement of science, art, or industry, and not intended for sale, shall be admitted free of duty, under such regulations as the Secretary of the Treasury shall prescribe; but bonds shall be given for the payment to the United States of such duties as may be imposed by law upon any and all of such articles as shall not be exported within six months after such importation: Provided that the Secretary of the Treasury may in his discretion extend such period for a further term of six months in cases where application therefor shall be made.

759. Works of art, collections in illustration of the progress of the arts, science, or manufactures, photographs, works in terra-cotta, parina, pottery, or porcelain, and artistic copies of antiquities in metal or other material hereafter imported in good faith for permanent exhibition at a fixed place by any society or institution established for the encouragement of the arts or of science, and all like articles imported in good faith by any society or association for the purpose of erecting a public monument and not intended for sale, nor for any other purpose than herein expressed; but bonds shall be given under such rules and regulations as the Secretary of the Treasury may prescribe for the payment of lawful duties which may accrue should any of the articles aforesaid be sold, transferred, or used contrary to this provision, and such articles shall be subject at any time to examination and inspection by the proper officers of the customs: provided that the privileges of this and the preceding section shall not be allowed to associations or corporations engaged in or connected with business of a private or commercial character.

The Law of Copyright.

EXTRACTS FROM THE REVISED STATUTES OF THE UNITED STATES, IN FORCE DECEMBER 1, 1873, AS AMENDED BY ACT APPROVED JUNE 18, 1874, AND BY ACT APPROVED MARCH 3, 1891, AND FROM THE PROCLAMATIONS OF PRESIDENT HARRISON.

SECTION 4948. All records and other things relating to copyrights and required by law to be preserved, shall be under the control of the Librarian of Congress, and kept and preserved in the Library of Congress.

SEC. 4952. The author, inventor, designer, or proprietor of any book, map, chart, dramatic or musical composition, engraving, cut, print, or photograph or negative thereof, or of a painting, drawing, chromo, statuary, and of models or designs intended to be perfected as works of the fine arts, and the executors, administrators, or assigns of any such person, shall, upon complying with the provisions of this chapter, have the sole liberty of printing, reprinting, publishing, completing, copying, executing, finishing, and vending the same; and, in the case of a dramatic composition, of publicly performing or representing it, or causing it to be performed or represented by others. And authors or their assigns shall have exclusive right to dramatize or translate any of their works, for which copyright shall have been obtained under the laws of the United States.

SEC. 4953. Copyrights shall be granted for the term of twenty-eight years from the time of recording the title thereof, in the manner hereinafter directed.

SEC. 4954. The author, inventor, or designer, if he be still living, or his widow or children, if he be dead, shall have the same exclusive right continued for the further term of fourteen years, upon recording the title of the work or description of the article so secured a second time, and complying with all other regulations in regard to original copyrights, within six months before the expiration of the first term. And such persons shall, within two months from the date of said renewal, cause a copy of the record thereof to be published in one or more newspapers, printed in the United States, for the space of four weeks.

SEC. 4955. Copyrights shall be assignable in law by any instrument of writing, and such assignment shall be recorded in the office of the Librarian of Congress within sixty days after its execution; in default of which it shall be void as against any subsequent purchaser or mortgagee for a valuable consideration, without notice.

SEC. 4956. No person shall be entitled to a copyright unless he shall, on or before the day of publication, in this or any foreign country, deliver at the office of the Librarian of Congress, or deposit in the mail within the United States, addressed to the Librarian of Congress, at Washington, District of Columbia, a printed copy of the title of the book, map, chart, dramatic or musical composition, engraving, cut, print, photograph, or chromo, or a description of the painting, drawing, statue, statuary, or a model or design, for a work of the fine arts, for which he desires a copyright; nor unless he shall also, not later than the day of the publication thereof, in this or any foreign country, deliver at the office of the Librarian of Congress, at Washington, District of Columbia, or deposit in the mail, within the United States, addressed to the Librarian of Congress, at Washington, District of Columbia, two copies of such copyright book, map, chart, dramatic or musical composition, engraving, chromo, cut, print, or photograph, or in case of a painting, drawing, statue, statuary, model, or design for a work of the fine arts, a photograph of the same: *Provided*, That in the case of a book, photograph, chromo, or lithograph, the two copies of the same, required to be delivered or deposited as above, shall be printed from type set within the limits of the United States, or from plates made therefrom, or from negatives, or drawings on stone made within the limits of the United States, or from transfers made therefrom. During the existence of such copyright the importation into the United States of any book, chromo, lithograph, or photograph, so copyrighted, or any edition or editions thereof, or any plates of the same not made from type set, negatives, or drawings on stone made within the limits of the United States, shall be, and it is hereby prohibited, except in the cases specified in paragraphs 512 to 516, inclusive, in section two of the act entitled an act to reduce the revenue and equalize the duties on imports and for other purposes, approved Oct. 1, 1890; and except in the case of persons purchasing for use and not for sale, who import, subject to the duty thereon, not more than two copies of such book at any one time; and, except in the case of newspapers and magazines, not containing in whole or in part matter copyrighted under the provisions of this act, unauthorized by the author which are hereby exempted from prohibition of importation.

SEC. 4957. The Librarian of Congress shall record the name

of such copyright book, or other article, forthwith in a book to be kept for that purpose, in the words following: "Library of Congress, to wit: Be it remembered that on the   day of   A. B., of   hath deposited in this office the title of a book (map, chart, or otherwise, as the case may be, or description of the article), the title or description of which is in the following words, to wit, (here insert the title or description,) the right whereof he claims as author (originator, or proprietor, as the case may be), in conformity with the laws of the United States respecting copyrights. C. D., Librarian of Congress." And he shall give a copy of the title or description, under the seal of the Librarian of Congress, to the proprietor, whenever he shall require it.

SEC. 4958. The Librarian of Congress shall receive from the persons to whom the services designated are rendered, the following fees: 1. For recording the title or description of any copyright book or other article, fifty cents. 2. For every copy under seal of such record actually given to the person claiming the copyright, or his assigns, fifty cents. 3. For recording and certifying any instrument of writing for the assignment of a copyright, one dollar. 4. For every copy of an assignment, one dollar. All fees so received shall be paid into the treasury of the United States: *Provided*, That the charge for recording the title or description of any article entered for copyright, the production of a person not a citizen or resident of the United States, shall be one dollar, to be paid as above into the treasury of the United States, to defray the expenses of lists of copyrighted articles as hereinafter provided.

SEC. 4959. The proprietor of every copyright book or other article shall deliver at the office of the Librarian of Congress, or deposit in the mail, addressed to the Librarian of Congress, at Washington, District of Columbia, a copy of every subsequent edition wherein any substantial changes shall be made: *Provided, however*, That the alterations, revisions, and additions made to books by foreign authors, heretofore published, of which new editions shall appear subsequently to the taking effect of this act, shall be held and deemed capable of being copyrighted as above provided for in this act, unless they form a part of the series in course of publication at the time this act shall take effect.

SEC. 4960. For every failure on the part of the proprietor of any copyright to deliver, or deposit in the mail, either of the published copies, or description, or photograph, required by Sections 4956 and 4959, the proprietor of the copyright shall be liable to a penalty of twenty-five dollars, to be recovered by the Librarian of Congress, in the name of the United States, in an action in the nature of an action of debt, in any district court of the United States within the jurisdiction of which the delinquent may reside or be found.

SEC. 4961. The postmaster to whom such copyright book, title, or other article is delivered, shall, if requested, give a receipt therefor; and when so delivered he shall mail it to its destination.

SEC. 4962. No person shall maintain an action for the infringement of his copyright unless he shall give notice thereof by inserting in the several copies of every edition published, on the titlepage, or the page immediately following, if it be a book; or if a map, chart, musical composition, print, cut, engraving, photograph, painting, drawing, chromo, statue, statuary, or model or design intended to be perfected and completed as a work of the fine arts, by inscribing upon some visible portion thereof, or of the substance on which the same shall be mounted, the following words, viz.: "Entered according to act of Congress, in the year ———, by A. B., in the office of the Librarian of Congress, at Washington"; or, at his option, the word "Copyright," together with the year the copyright was entered, and the name of the party by whom it was taken out, thus: "Copyright, 18—, by A. B."

SEC. 4963. Every person who shall insert or impress such notice, or words of the same purport, in or upon any book, map, chart, dramatic or musical composition, print, cut, engraving, or photograph, or other article, for which he has not obtained a copyright, shall be liable to a penalty of one hundred dollars, recoverable one half for the person who shall sue for such penalty, and one half to the use of the United States.

SEC. 4964. Every person who, after the recording of the title of any book and the depositing of two copies of such book as provided by this act, shall, contrary to the provisions of this act, within the term limited, and without the consent of the proprietor of the copyright first obtained in writing, signed in presence of two or more witnesses, print, publish, dramatize, translate, or import, or, knowing the same to be so printed, published, dramatized, translated, or imported, shall sell or expose to sale any copy of such book, shall forfeit every copy thereof to such proprietor, and shall also forfeit and pay such damages as may be recovered in a civil action by such proprietor in any court of competent jurisdiction.

SEC. 4965. If any person, after the recording of the title of any map, chart, dramatic or musical composition, print, cut, engraving, or photograph, or cromo, or of the description of any painting, drawing, statue, statuary, or model or design intended to be perfected and executed as a work of the fine arts as provided by this act, shall, within the term limited, contrary to the provisions of this act, and without the consent of the proprietor of the copyright first obtained in writing, signed in presence of two or more witnesses, engrave, etch, work, copy, print, publish, dramatize, translate, or import, either in whole or in part, or by varying the main design, with intent to evade the law, or, knowing the same to be so printed, published, dramatized, translated, or imported, shall sell or expose to sale any copy of such map or other article, as aforesaid, he shall forfeit to the proprietor all the plates on which the same shall be copied, and every sheet thereof, either copied or printed, and shall further forfeit one dollar for every sheet of the same found in his possession, either printing, printed, copied, published, imported, or exposed for sale; and in case of a painting, statue, or statuary, he shall forfeit ten dollars for every copy of the same in his possession, or by him sold or exposed for sale: one half thereof to the proprietor and the other half to the use of the United States.

SEC. 4966. Any person publicly performing or representing any dramatic composition for which a copyright has been obtained, without the consent of the proprietor thereof, or his heirs or assigns, shall be liable for damages therefor: such damages in all cases to be assessed at such sum, not less than one hundred dollars for the first, and fifty dollars for every subsequent performance, as to the court shall appear just.

SEC. 4967. Every person who shall print or publish any manuscript whatever, without the consent of the author or proprietor first obtained, shall be liable to the author or proprietor for all damages occasioned by such injury.

SEC. 4968. No action shall be maintained in any case of forfeiture or penalty under the copyright laws, unless the same is commenced within two years after the cause of action has arisen.

SEC. —[Approved June 18, 1874, to take effect August 1, 1874.] In the construction of this act the words "engraving," "cut," and "print," shall be applied only to pictorial illustrations of works connected with the fine arts, and no prints or labels designed to be used for any other articles of manufacture shall be entered under the copyright law, but may be registered in the Patent Office

SEC. 11 [Approved March 3, 1891, to take effect July 1, 1891.] That for the purpose of this act each volume of a book in two or more volumes, when such volumes are published separately, and the first one shall not have been issued before this act shall take effect, and each number of a periodical shall be considered an independent publication, subject to the form of copyrighting as above.

SEC. 13. [Approved March 3, 1891, to take effect July 1, 1891.] That this act shall only apply to a citizen or subject of a foreign state or nation when such foreign state or nation permits to citizens of the United States of America the benefit of copyright

Art Publishing Co.,

132 Boylston Street,
Boston.

on substantially the same basis as its own citizens; or when such foreign state or nation is a party to an international agreement which provides for reciprocity in the grant of copyright, by the terms of which agreement the United States of America may at its pleasure become a party to such agreement. The existence of either of the conditions aforesaid shall be determined by the President of the United States, by proclamation made from time to time as the purposes of this act may require.

Satisfactory official assurances having been given that in Belgium, France, Great Britain, and the British Possessions and Switzerland, the law permits to citizens of the United States the benefit of copyright in substantially the same basis as to the citizens of those countries, copyright benefits were extended to citizens of those countries by President Harrison July 1, 1891. April 15, 1892 they were extended to German subjects.

WADSWORTH, HOWLAND & CO.,

MANUFACTURERS OF

Artists' Oil and Water Colors,

Varnishes, Brushes, Palettes, Easels, etc.

IMPORTERS AND DEALERS IN

ARTISTS' AND DRAFTSMEN'S SUPPLIES.

CATALOGUE MAILED FREE.

82 and 84 Washington St.,

BOSTON.

Factories: Malden, Mass.

Foster Brothers,

IMPORTERS OF

Etchings, Engravings, Photographs, etc.

MANUFACTURERS OF
ARTISTIC PICTURE FRAMES,

164 Boylston Street,

BOSTON.

Factory, 185 Cambridge Street.

Massachusetts Artists Represented at the Columbian Exposition at Chicago.

Thomas Allen.
Hugo Breul.
Caroline Bunker.
Max Bachmann.
M. K. Baker.
E. H. Barnard.
F. W. Benson.
E. C. Cabot.
L. H. Caliga.
W. W. Churchill, Jr.
J. G. Cochrane.
Lucy S. Conant.
C. A. Cranch.
C. H. Davis.
W. L. Dean.
E. S. Dixey.
A. W. Dow.
D. Jerome Elwell.
J. J. Enneking.
Lucia Fairchild.
F. W. Freer.
I. M. Gaugengigl.
Abbott Graves.
Lilian Green.
Walter Gay.
J. H. Greenwood.
H. R. Hyatt.
B. D. Hodgkins.
E. D. W. Hamilton.
Ellen D. Hale.
H. H. Hallett.
M. Hallowell.
J. M. Hammond.
M. H. Hardwick.
J. B. Hatfield.
Charles H. Hayden.
Edith M. Howes.
E. L. Ipsen.
Anna E. Klumpe.
Louis Kronberg.
F. M. Lamb.
C. W. Lathrop.
Laura Lee.
E. L. Major.
A. H. Munsell.
E. G. Niles.
S. Mary Norton.
W. E. Norton.
—— Norcross.
J. A. Pritchard.
William O. Partridge.

W. M. Paxton.
C. S. Pearce.
S. D. Peralta.
Lilla Cabot Perry.
C. F. Pierce.
S. G. Putnam.
F. H. Richardson.
Arthur Rotch.
Theo Alice Ruggles.
H. O. Ryder.
J. L. Smith.
Alice Stackpole.
J. M. Stone.
M. Silsbee.
E. E. Simmons.
E. C. Tarbell.
F. W. Tewksbury.
Stacy Tolman.
F. H. Tompkins.
Ross Turner.
F. P. Vinton.
Sarah W. Whitman.
Charles H. Woodbury.
A. E. Wadsworth.
Jacob Wagner.
F. E. Wesselhoeft.
M. L. Brown.
W. P. Cleaves.
W. B. Closson.
W. J. Dana.
F. E. Fillebrown.
R. Lovenell.
H. E. W. Lyons.
J. A. S. Monks.
S. A. Scoff.
H. E. Sylvester.
C. A. Walker.
Andrews, Jacques & Rantoul.
H. Langford Warren.
Wheelwright & Haven.
Peabody & Stearns.
Sturgis & Cabot.
George P. Fernald.
E. M. Wheelwright.
Cram, Wentworth & Goodhue.
C. Howard Walker.
R. Clipson Sturgis.
Walker & Kimball.
Longfellow, Alden & Harlow.
Rotch & Tilden.
J. A. Schweinfurth.

BOSTON ART GUIDE.

Mr. ROSS TURNER,

Classes in Water Color, Painting, Still Life and Models.

TUESDAY AND FRIDAY MORNINGS.

For terms and information, apply to 248 Boylston Street, opposite Public Garden, Boston, Mass.

Miss FANNY W. TEWKSBURY,

Studio, 212 Boylston St.,

BOSTON.

LESSONS IN WATER COLORS.　　Summer class at East Gloucester, Mass.
Tuesday afternoons.

WM. W. CHURCHILL, Jr.

Harcourt Building, Room 19,　-　-　-　Irvington Street, Boston.

Receives Saturday afternoons, 2 until 4.

Receives pupils in oil painting from life and in landscape painting at Kennebunkport, Maine, during the summer months.

Miss HELEN M. KNOWLTON,

23 IRVINGTON STREET.

Teacher of drawing and painting from nature and from life. Oils, pastels, and water colors.

Receives on Thursdays, 2.30 to 4.30.

H. PEABODY FLAGG,

Room 54, Studio Building,　-　-　-　Boston.

Saturday afternoons.

Mr. DANIEL J. STRAIN,

Portraits and Figures in Oil,

278 BOYLSTON STREET.

Reception Days, Saturdays.

WALTER F. LANSIL.　　WILBUR H. LANSIL.

MARINE AND CATTLE PAINTING.

Studio Building, 110 Tremont St., Room 56.

List of Artists and Studio Addresses.

Adams, C. L., 248 Boylston St.
Adams, W. Loring, 21 Pemberton Sq.
Allen, Mary C., 61 Pierce Building.
Allen, Thomas, 12 Commonwealth Ave.
Ames, E. F., 170 Tremont St., room 10.
Andrews, H. N., 180 Tremont St., room 32.
Attwill, E. B., 149 A Tremont St.
Attwood, F. G., Greenwood Ave., J. P.
Auerbach, T., 37 Broadway Extension.
Babcock, W. G., Jr., Clarkson St., Dorchester.
Bacon, Fred W., 31 A Boylston St.
Badger, T. H., 11 Akron St.
Bailey, R. M., Jr., 12 West St., room 29.
Bailey, Mercy, Hotel Pelham, 84 Boylston St.
Baker, M. K., Miss, 47 Studio Building.
Barnard, E. H., 23 Irvington St., studio 16.
Bass, Mrs. E. E., 524 Tremont St.
Barrows, Mrs. A. B., 1 Oxford Terrace.
Bartlett, George H., 27 Tremont Row.
Bartlett, Miss M. E., 5 Park St.
Bartlett, Jane E., 23 Irvington St., studio 13.
Bartol, E. H., Miss, 17 Chestnut St.
Beal, H. M., 12 West St.
Bennett, Mr. M. F., 22 Pemberton Sq.
Bennett, Cecilia, 131 Tremont St.
Bennett, M. C., 131 Tremont St.
Benson, Frank, 23 Irvington St., studio 12.
Bicknell, W. H. W., Winchester, Mass.
Billings, E. T., 55 Studio Building.
Bixbee, William J., 22 School St.
Blair, G. H., 16 Mt. Vernon St.
Blake, Miss A. D., 94 Chestnut St.
Blaney, H. L., 8 Follen St.
Blaney, Mrs. H. Farley, 8 Follen St.
Borris, Albert, Wren, near Oriole St.
Boyle, N. D., Mrs., 72 Huntington Ave.
Brackett, S. Lawrence, 616 Washington St.
Brackett, Walter M., 41 Tremont St.
Bradford, Miss M. A., 30 Studio Building.
Brainard, E. H., Mrs., 2 Park Sq.

KARL von RYDINGSVÄRD.
(BARON VON PROSCHWITZ.)

School of Artistic Wood Carving and Sculpture.

Special Classes for Ladies, Monday, Thursday, and Friday, 10 to 12 A. M.
Ladies are cordially invited to visit the Studio during class hours.
2 PARK SQUARE, BOSTON.

LOUIS KRONBERG,
STUDIO, 246 BOYLSTON STREET, BOSTON.

Oils and Pastels.

10 to 1, 2.30 to 4.
Receives Saturday Afternoons.

J. J. ENNEKING.

Studio, 174 Tremont Street, Boston.

Landscapes in Oil.

ELLEN A. RICHARDSON,

Tiles.   -   -   Limoges Underglaze.   -   -   Vases.

OPAQUE WATER-COLORS ON CANVAS.

Lesson mornings, Tuesdays and Fridays.

STUDIO, 57 PIERCE BUILDING,   OFFICE, No 56.
Copley Square.   1 to 4 P. M.

Miss AGNES LEAVITT

Will receive Pupils in Oil and Water-Color Painting at her Studio,

159 A Tremont Street - Boston.

CECILIA BENNETT'S STUDIO,
131 TREMONT STREET.

Classes in China Painting daily from 9 to 12 A. M., and 1 to 4 P. M. Wednesday afternoon excepted. Agency for the Studio Kilns.

TERMS.—Single Lessons, including all materials except china and gold, $1.50. Terms of eight lessons, $10.00.

Receives Wednesday afternoons.

Miss J. M. SCUDDER and Miss S. W. HATHAWAY,
STUDIO 58, 2 PARK SQUARE.

Classes in Oil, Water Color, and Charcoal. Outdoor Sketching after May 1.

Receptions Saturday afternoons.

Breck, J. L., Mechanics' Building.
Breen, James T., 31 Pemberton Sq.
Breul, Hugo, 12 West St., room 29.
Bridgman, L. J., 27 School St.
Brown, H. L., Miss, 82 Studio Building.
Brown, J. R., Everett, Mass.
Browne, Francis, 107 Tremont St.
Bryant, Wallace, 2 Commonwealth Ave.
Buhler, Augustus, 104 Dartmouth St.
Burgess, H. George, 616 Washington St.
Burpee, William P., 23 Irvington St.
Burrage, C. E., Miss, Mechanics' Building, 135 Huntington Ave., studio 6.
Butland, J. L., Mrs., 54 Kilby St., room 9.
Caliga, I. H., 174 Tremont St.
Caldwell, C. W., 180 Tremont St.
Campbell, Miss L. S., 3 Oxford Terrace.
Cardell, F. H., 125 Tremont St.
Carlson, Emile, 12 West St.
Carpenter, Elles M., 214 Columbus Ave.
Champney, Benjamin, 21 Bromfield St.
Childs, Miss, 2 Park Sq.
Churchill, W. W., Jr., Harcourt Building, studio 19.
Clark, E. B., 133 Dorchester Ave.
Claus, W. A. J., New England Conservatory of Music.
Cobb, F. W., 244 Tremont St.
Cobb, Darius, 22 Pemberton Sq.
Cole, Adelaide, 304 Boylston St.
Comins, L. B., Miss, 304 Boylston St.
Conlin, F. B., 37 Winter St.
Cook, Henry, 53 Studio Building.
Coolidge, J. T., Jr., 114 Beacon St.
Copeland, Charles, Studio Building, room 49.
Corbett, A., Jr., 54 Kilby St.
Cowdery, E. D., Mrs., Hotel Pelham.
Cowles, F. M., 145 Dartmouth St.
Cowles, J. E., 145 Dartmouth St.
Cox, Albert S., 27 School St., room 77.
Crosby, H. A., Mrs., 149 A Tremont St.
Curtis, Alice M., Miss, 264 Boylston St.
Dabney, Miss Julia P., 37 West Cedar St.
Dalrymple, Miss Amy F., 257 Emerson St.
Dana, C. G., 180 Tremont St.
Davis, Mrs. M M., 57 West Cedar St.
Day, Henry, 149 A Tremont St., room 63.
Dean, Walter L., 2 Pemberton Sq.
DeBlois, F. B., 48 Winter St., room 16.

ARTISTS' MATERIALS

... FOR ...

Crayon and Charcoal Drawing, China, Oil, and Water-Color Drawing.

Art Manuals on all subjects, Etching Materials, Studies of all kinds, Mathematical Instruments, Architects' and Engineers' Supplies, etc.

Picture Framing in all Styles.

BLUE PRINTS AND BLUE PRINT PAPERS.

FROST & ADAMS, Importers,

37 CORNHILL, - - BOSTON, MASS.

Miss LILLIAN WALKER,
TEACHER OF

TAPESTRY DYE PAINTING,

... DRAWING, OIL AND WATER COLORS. ...

CHINA PAINTING *WITHOUT TURPENTINE.*

ORDERS EXECUTED.

Fancy Novelties at Holiday Season.

Room 41, 110 Tremont St., - - Boston, Mass.

C. W. CALDWELL,

Crayon Portraits,

180 TREMONT ST., - - ROOM 36,

BOSTON.

DeCamp, J. R., Mechanics' Building, 135 Huntington Ave.
Dickerman, Albert, 40 Chester Pk.
Dodge, S. E., 671 Washington St.
Dole, Mrs. E. F., 36 Hancock St.
Dow, A. W., Stone Building, cor. Boylston and Exeter Sts.
Downs, Albert E., 449 E. Third St.
Duffee, P. Edwin, 19 Tremont Row.
Durgin, H., Miss, Pierce Building, Copley Sq.
Durgin, Lyle, Pierce Building, Copley Sq.
Dustin, G. F., 112 Berkeley St.
Dziekonska, Kasimir, Mlle., 98 Boylston St.
Eaton, Clarissa, Miss, River St., near Hyde Park line, Mat.
Edmands, Miss, 2 Park Sq.
Eksergian, C., 175 Tremont St., room 69.
Eldred, L. D., 76 Studio Building.
Elliott, Harriet F., 180 Tremont St.
Ellis, Lucy, 154 Tremont St.
Emerson, C. C., 2 Park Sq.
England, W. A., 51 Falmouth St.
Enneking, John J., 174 Tremont St.
Fennety, A. C., 180 Tremont St.
Fennety, F. M., 84 Studio Building.
Field, L. B., 120 Tremont St.
Flagg, H. Peabody, 54 Studio Building.
Fletcher, Gilbert S., 60½ West Cedar St.
Fletcher, Harold, 149 A Tremont St.
Folsom, V. B., 68 Studio Building.
French, Julia M., Miss, 284 Boylston St.
Gallagher, Sears, 3 Winter St.
Gannett, E. H., Winchester.
Gaugengigl, I. M., 45 Studio Building.
George, Vesper L., 166 Boylston St.
Gibbons, M. A., 118 Essex St.
Gilbert, James, 32 Studio Building.
Giles, H. P., 146 Tremont St.
Gillingham, Miss Annie M., 5 Park St.
Goodwin, Miss E. F., 2304 Washington St.
Gray, M. S., 23 Winter St.
Gregory, Miss A. M., 78 Berkeley St.
Green, C. E. L., 34 School St.
Green, Miss Lilian, 23 Irvington St.
Greyer, L. A., 25 Bromfield St.
Griggs, S. W., 63 Studio Building.
Guild, S., 254 Beacon St.
Hale, E. D., Miss, 8 Park St.
Hale, Martha, Miss, 4 Pemberton Sq.

JULIA ARDELLE SPRAGUE,

Instruction in China and Glass Decoration.

China on sale at RAND & CRANE'S, 3 PARK STREET.

STUDIO AT 2 PARK SQUARE.

China and Glass Decoration and Water Colors.

LESSONS GIVEN BY

Mrs. C. L. Swift, - Studio, 2 Park Sq.

Mrs. MARY C. ALLEN,

Studio, Pierce Building, Copley Sq., Boston, Mass.

Fridays from 2 to 6.

CHINA DECORATION.

Lessons given in all styles of China Decoration by Miss JULIA PERRIN. Class Days, Tuesday, Wednesday and Saturday.

Park Building, Park Sq.

C. FREDERICK VILLIERS,

From the Royal Academy of Arts, London, England, and Paris.
180 TREMONT STREET.

Portraits in Oils and Pastels.

Lessons in Portraits, Figures and Landscapes. Pupils in private lessons and in classes. Reception on Thursday afternoon from 2 until 5.

SID L. BRACKETT,

616 Washington Street, corner Essex.

Portraits of Animals,

AND INSTRUCTION IN ANIMAL PAINTING.

FRED C. CLARKE,

DESIGNER AND ILLUSTRATOR,

110 Tremont St., Room 39, Boston.

Hale, M., 23 Irvington St.
Haley, L. M., Hotel Berkeley.
Hallett, Hendricks A., 42 Court St., room 34.
Hallowell, G. H., 356 Boylston St.
Hallowell, Miss M., 284 Boylston St.
Halsall, W. F., 174 Tremont St.
Hamilton, E. D., 162 Boylston St.
Hanlon, E. L., 122 Boylston St.
Hardie, James Gordon, 145 Dartmouth St.
Hardie, R. G., 145 Boylston St.
Hardwick, M. H., 12 West St., room 11.
Harris, George W., 8 Braintree St., room 11.
Haskell, Miss J. P., 27 School St.
Hathaway, Miss, 2 Park Sq.
Hayden, C. H., 23 Irvington St., studio 4.
Henry, A. M., Mrs., 1 Mt. Vernon St.
Higgins, George F., 26 Studio Building.
Highwood, C., 127 Tremont St.
Hinds, Miss Helen M., 11 Hamilton Place, room 15.
Holden, H. A., Mrs., 77 Boylston St.
Holmes, S. J., Mrs., 10 Fountain St.
Howard, Mary W., Mrs., 3 Winter St.
Howe, G. W., 32 Ruggles St.
Hudson, C. W., 13 Hilton St., Hyde Park.
Hyams, Sarah, 179 Tremont St.
Jackson, William H., 50 Bromfield St., room 29.
Jarvis, Miss M., 180 Tremont St.
Jenks, Miss Phœbe A., 52 Studio Building.
Jenkins, Miss J. W., 83 Sudbury St.
Johnson, Marshall, Jr., 12 West St., room 26.
Johnston, S. J., 154 Tremont St.
Kaan, Emma, 23 Irvington St., studio 10.
Keep, A. M., 127 A Tremont St.
Kendrick, D. T., Wren St.
Kingman, F., 22 School St.
Knowlton, H. M., 23 Irvington St., studio 17.
Knox, Edw., 6 Winthrop Block, East Boston.
Kronberg, L., 246 Boylston St.
Lackey, H. G., 67 Studio Building.
Lane, Harry E., 179 Tremont St., room 1.
Langerfeldt, T. O., 129 Charles St.
Lansil, W. F., 56 Studio Building.
Lansil, W. H., 56 Studio Building.
Lanza, Miss M. P., 22 West Cedar St.
Leavitt, Miss Agnes M., 159 A Tremont St.
Lee, Laura, Miss, 23 Irvington St.
Leganger, N. T., 51 Summer St.

C. W. SANDERSON,
Lessons Given in Water Color,
20 BEACON STREET.

First of November to first of June.

G. W. SEAVEY,

28 Studio Building, • • • • • • • Boston, Mass.

DURING THE WINTER MONTHS.

Ponce de Leon Studios, • • • • • St. Augustine, Florida.

Fridays.

Mr. J. A. S. MONKS
Will receive pupils in Water Color Painting.
STUDIO, 12 WEST STREET.

Miss ANNIE C. NOWELL,
Studio, 180 Tremont Street, Room 33.
WATER AND PASTEL PORTRAITS.

Afternoons.

EMMA F. GOODWIN,
Studio, 2304 WASHINGTON STREET, ROXBURY.

Water Colors, China Decoration, Cast Drawing.

Mondays, 2 to 4 P. M.

F. EVELYN NUTE,
Portraits.

PUPILS IN CRAYON AND PASTEL.   60 STUDIO BUILDING.

Wednesday afternoons.

FREDERIC D. WILLIAMS,
23 IRVINGTON STREET.

Landscapes in Oil and Water Colors.

At home every afternoon from 2 to 4 P. M.

Receives a few pupils.

Leighton, Scott, 3 Winter St.
Litchfield, C. M., 523 Washington St.
Little, W. J., 135 Huntington Ave.
Loring, G. A., 66 Studio Building.
Low, Gilman, Studio Building.
Ludoviga, Mlle., 6 Winter St.
Lugves, Frank A., 246 Boylston St.
Lyman, Charlotte A., 59 Hancock St.
Lyndon, W. M., 512 Tremont St.
Major, Ernest L., 145 Dartmouth St.
Marr, T. E., 180 Tremont St.
Martin, C. H., 81 Boylston St.
Martin, L. Edna, Miss, 88 Boylston St.
McCall, James, 3 Tremont Row.
McGurk, Mrs. M. C., 29 Studio Building.
McKay, Mrs., 12 School St.
McLean, W. D., 21 Pemberton Sq.
McNeil, Fred A., 31 Pemberton Sq.
Menard, Miss N., 85 Studio Building.
Merrill, F. T., 16 Tremlett St.
Merrow, C. E. A., 521 Washington St.
Meynelle, Louis, 616 Washington St.
Miles, Samuel S., 85 Studio Building.
Mills, Chas. E., 135 Huntington Ave.
Monks, J. A. S., 12 West St.
Moore, Alice E., 27 School St.
Moulton & Barry, Misses, Hotel Pelham.
Moulton, Frank, 709 E. Fourth St.
Munsell, Albert H., 132 Boylston St.
Myrick, Frank, 28 School St.
Newcomb, Harry H., 179 Tremont St.
Niles, G. E., 329 Beacon St.
Niles, W. J., 98 Pinckney St.
Noa, Miss Alwina, 2 Park Sq.
Noa, Mrs. Jessie, 2 Park Sq.
Noah, Miss A. M., 27 School St.
Norton, Miss M. S., 297 Marlboro St.
Notman, G. S., Studio Building.
Nowell, Miss Annie C., 180 Tremont St.
Nute, Miss F. E., 60 Studio Building.
Ordway, Alfred, 51 Studio Building.
Osgood, L. S., Mechanics' Building.
Page, Hollis Bowman, Chestnut Hill.
Page, E. E., 2 Park Sq.
Palmer, Miss Adelaide, 149 A Tremont St.
Parker, C. S., 228 Commonwealth Ave.
Parker, Edgar, 3 Winter St.

ART SUPPLY DEPARTMENT.

Artists

..AND..

Scholars

SUPPLIED AT

CUT PRICES

WITH

Our Specialties.

High Grade
        Canvas,
All Standard
        Artist Colors,
    Sketching Outfits,
Fine Art Studies,
    Pencils and Brushes,
        China Colors,
Sketching Umbrellas,   Materials,
    Sketching Stools,
        Easels, Color Boxes, etc.

ALL THE LATEST ART PUBLICATIONS.

Books and Drawing Materials.

HOLLANDER,   }   PUBLIC STORES.
BRADSHAW,   615 Washington St.
FOLSOM,

Parsons, Lydia A., 27 School St.
Paskell, W. F., 1 Lonsdale Terrace.
Peabody, John E., 161 Tremont St.
Peralta, Mme. F. de, " The Ludlow," St. James Ave.
Perkins, S. E., 86 Studio Building.
Perrin, Miss Julia A., 2 Park Sq.
Pierce, H. W., 47 Studio Building.
Pierce, C. F., 12 West St.
Pinkham, Mrs. A. J., 35 Waltham St.
Plaisted, Miss Z. M., 6 Beacon St.
Platt, Miss M. A., 81 Studio Building.
Plumer, Miss N. D., 149 A Tremont St.
Pope, Alexander, 23 Irvington St.
Pope, Arthur E., 120 Tremont St.
Pope, Miss Edith, 27 School St.
Porter, Mrs. A. E., 72 Studio Building.
Porter, Edwin F., 34 School St.
Prichard, J. A., 175 Tremont St.
Raymond, Miss H. T., Mechanics' Building.
Reed, E. R., 469 Tremont St.
Remick, Mrs. E. S., 42 Studio Building.
Rice, H. W., 23 Irvington St.
Rich, J. Rogers, The Charlesgate.
Rich, J. R., 167 Tremont St.
Richardson, F. H., 23 Irvington St.
Richardson, E. A., 57 Pierce Building.
Richards, M. M., 180 Tremont St.
Robbins, Miss Ellen, 6 Beacon St.
Robinson, Catharine, 132 Boylston St.
Roos, Peter, 270 Boylston St.
Russ, Harry, 246 Boylston St.
Ryder, John S., 2557 Washington St.
Rydingsvärd, Karl von, 2 Park Sq.
Sanderson, C. W., 20 Beacon St.
Sandham, H., 152 Boylston St.
Santry, Daniel F., 12 West St.
Scroff, A. H., 3 Tremont Row.
Scroff, H., 3 Tremont Row.
Scudder, Miss J. M., 2 Park Sq.
Sears, Mrs. S. M., 22 Blagden St.
Seavey, G. W., 28 Studio Building.
Selinger, Mrs. Emily, 3 Hamilton Pl.
Selinger, J. P., 3 Hamilton Pl.
Severence, Minot F., 145 Dartmouth St.
Sequitz, Fred, 125 Tremont St.
Shapleigh, F. H., 79 Studio Building.
Shaw, F. A., 23 Irvington St.

Cowles Art School,

NEW STUDIO BUILDING,

145 Dartmouth Street,

BOSTON.

♣

INSTRUCTORS:

Ernest L. Major, *Mercy A. Bailey,*
Joseph DeCamp, *Theo. A. Ruggles,*
Henry H. Kitson, *Annie E. Riddell,*
Bertram G. Goodhue.

♣

J. E. COWLES, Secretary.

Mrs. ELIZABETH M. REED, Asst. Secretary.

♣

VISITORS:

I. M. Gaugengigl,   *Charles E. Mills,*
J. Templeman Coolidge, Jr.

♣

FRANK M. COWLES, Manager.

♣

The eleventh year will open October 1, 1893. The only school in Boston in which life and modelling classes are made the only prominent feature. The drawing and painting classes consist of men's and women's morning life classes, morning and afternoon head classes, evening life, morning and evening antique, modelling from life and antique, water colors, still life, illustrating, perspective, artistic anatomy compositions. Begin any time. Five hundred dollars in scholarships. Free access to galleries of the Museum of Fine Arts.

Sheridan, Miss K. E.
Shute, Augustus B., 12 West St.
Silloway, Anna H., 75 Studio Building.
Skinner, Mrs. E. C., 6 Park Sq.
Skowkowski, C. V., 36 Bromfield St.
Small, F. O., 31 Pinckney St.
Smith, Ambrose A., 168 Tremont St.
Smith, M. E., 12 School St.
Smith, Alfred E., 120 Boylston St.
Southworth, Miss Fannie B., 695 Washington St.
Sperry, J. H., 226 Tremont St.
Sprague, Miss Julia A., 2 Park Sq.
Starbuck, Miss F. M., 630 Centre St., J. P.
Stetson, J. B., 1164 Washington St.
Stillings, S. Vinton, 33 Boylston St.
Stone, J. M., 23 Irvington St.
Storer, Charles, 25 Bromfield St.
Strain, Daniel J., 278 Boylston St.
Strong, Beulah, 280 Boylston St.
Stubbs, W. P., 3 Bradstreet Ct.
Sturdevant, Miss A. L., 41 Pierce Building, Copley Sq.
Swift, Mrs. C. L., 2 Park Sq.
Tarbell, E. C., 23 Irvington St.
Taylor, W. L., Parley Vale, Dorchester.
Tewksbury, Miss F. W., 212 Boylston St.
Tolman, Stacy, 88 Boylston St.
Tompkins, F. H., 398 Northampton.
Triscott, S. P. R., 3 Winter St.
Turner, C. H., 192 Boylston St.
Turner, Ross, 248 Boylston St.
Villiers, C. F., 180 Tremont St.
Vinton, F. P., 17 Exeter St.
Vogel, Herman, 69 Studio Building.
Walker, Miss Lilian, 11 Studio Building.
Watkins, Miss K., Mechanics' Building.
Wagner, J., 23 Irvington St.
Waterman, Marcus, 616 Washington St.
Webber, Miss Florence I., 58 Studio Building.
Wenige, G., 26 Village St.
Wendell, T. M., Mechanics' Building.
Webber, Wesley, 1 Pemberton Sq.
Weeden, G. A., 72 Studio Building.
Whipple, Charles A., 142 Tremont St.
White, Sarah D., 12 West St.
Whitman, Mrs. H., 184 Boylston St.
Williams, F. D., 23 Irvington St.
Wright, F. E., 5 Park St.

HENRY R. BLANEY,

ETCHER ON COPPER,

8 Follen Street - - Boston.

. . . Etched linea reproductions of Paintings. . . .

Pen and Ink Illustration. Original Water Colors.

PUBLISHER OF 250 ORIGINAL ETCHINGS.

Catalogue mailed on application.

Sketches in the West Indies and New England.   Pupils received.

Mrs. HELEN FARLEY-BLANEY ART CLASSES,

PICTORIAL AND INDUSTRIAL,

103 TREMONT STREET, AND 8 FOLLEN STREET.

Opp. 69 Botolph St., Back Bay, Near Mechanics' Fair Building, Boston.

Scientific and Popular Courses in Form Study,
Drawing and Painting.
Illustration by Pen and Ink or Brush Work.
Etching on Copper and Design.

School Teachers and Art Students, wishing professional coaching or assistance, are invited to examine the methods.
There are also classes for ladies or children who wish to paint merely for diversion.
Lessons by correspondence.

GOLD.   **THE BEST MADE.**   **GOLD.**

CERAMIC GOLD WORKS,

MANUFACTURERS OF

Pure and Colored Golds, Bronzes, Oils, Colors and Brushes

FOR

China Decorating.

Send $1.00 for two Sample Boxes of Roman Gold. One Roman, one Green. Regular Price $2.00. Remit by Postal Note, P. O. Order, or Draft on Boston or New York.

NOTICE.—A full line of ART INTERCHANGE STUDIES for China Decoration, Oil and Water Color Painting, always in stock.

OFFICE: Pelham Building, cor. Boylston and Tremont Sts., Boston, Mass.

FACTORY AND KILNS AT HYDE PARK, MASS.   **T. A. WALTER, Manager.**

Wood, Miss A. B., 31 Berwick Park.
Woodbury, Chas. H., 175 Tremont St.
Woodbury, Mrs , 175 Tremont St.
Wyer, Miss E., 29 Studio Building.
Young, J. Harvey, 12 West St.

Sculptor.

Krams, Robert, Mechanics' Building.

A. DaPRATO & CO.

Florentine Statuary.

Importers and Manufacturers of

Artistic and Classical Subjects,

DECORATION VASES,

Art School Supplies, Ornamental Plaster Centre Pieces, etc.

13 and 14 Waverley House,

CHARLESTOWN DISTRICT,

BOSTON, MASS.

Architects.

Allen, F. R., 220 Devonshire St.
Andrews, Jacques & Rantoul, 8 Beacon St.
Appleton, Daniel, 220 Devonshire St.
Atkinson, Wm., 31 Milk St.
Atwood, H. H., 53 State St.
Austin, W. D., 6 Beacon St.
Avery, Geo. A., 82 Devonshire St.
Bacon, Willard M., 85 Water St.
Ballantine, G. A., 3 Pemberton Sq.
Ball & Dabney, 9 Park St.
Bateman, Chas. J., 7 Exchange Pl.
Beal, C. R., 209 Washington St.
Beal, J. W., 70 Kilby St.
Besarick, J. H., 33 Bedford St.
Besarick, Wm. H., 43 Milk St.
Blackall, C. H., Music Hall Building.
Blaikie, E. K. & W. E., 53 State St.
Boyden, E. N., 35 Congress St.
Bosworth, H. H., " The Ludlow."
Brazillian, James, 257 Washington St.
Briggs, L., 79 Milk St.
Brigham, Chas. H., 22 Beacon St.
Brown, J. Merrill, 53 State St.
Brown, Samuel J., 35 Congress St.
Bryant, G. J., 28 State St.
Cabot, Everett & Mead, 60 Devonshire St.
Cahill, George A., Woolsey blk., J. P.
Capen, G. Walter, 45 Kilby St.
Chamberlain & Whidden, 6 Beacon St.
Chapman & Frazer, 89 State St.
Clark, Eugene L., 50 Bromfield St.
Clark, George R., 132 Boylston St.
Clark, H. Paston, 110 Tremont St.
Clark, T. M., 22 Congress St.
Clark, Wm. E., 563 Main St., Cambridge.
Clough, C. A. E., City Hall.
Clough, George A., 33 Bedford St.
Codman, O., Jr., 100 Chestnut St.
Coit, Robert, 113 Devonshire St.

ALFRED SELLERS,

MANUFACTURER OF

Zinc, Copper and Brass Plates for Photo-Engravers.

TRANSFER ETCHING INK, INKING ROLLERS, PRINTING FRAMES, ETCHING TUBS, ENG. CHARCOAL, CHEMICALS, FORMULAS, ETC. . . . . .

Engravers' Steel and Copper Plates.

STEEL AND BRASS MONOGRAM DIES, WEDDING, VISITING, AND BUSINESS COPPER PLATES, ALSO ENGRAVERS' GENERAL SUPPLIES. . . . . . .

SEND FOR ILLUSTRATED CATALOGUE.

58 Fulton Street,

NEW YORK, N. Y.

Cole & Chandler, 120 Boylston St.
Copeland, F. W., 22 Chapman Pl.
Couch, L. S., 70 Kilby St.
Cram, Wentworth & Goodhue, 53 State St.
Dahl, John, 142 P. O. Building.
Darrow, A. L., 113 Devonshire St.
Deane, E. Eldon, 29 Pemberton Sq.
Dwight, B. F., 144 Tremont St.
Eastman, J. S., 16 Decatur St., E. B.
Eaton, J. F., 28 State St.
Emerson, Wm. R., 85 Water St.
Faxon, Jno. Lyman, 7 Exchange Pl.
Fehmer & Page, 87 Milk St.
Footman, F. N., 12 Pearl St.
Ford, P. W., 657 Washington St.
Forrest, A. L., 4 Pemberton Sq.
Fox, Jno. A., 120 Tremont St.
Fox, J. A., 218 Boylston St.
Frost, Willard A., 120 Tremont St.
Frink, A., 28 State St.
Fuller, George F., 14 State St.
Gale, E. J., 218 Boylston St.
Goodwin, Wm., 5 Tremont St.
Gould & Angell, 31 Milk St.
Graham, A. M., 178 Devonshire St.
Gray, A. F., 53 State St.
Griffin, T., 172 Washington St.
Hall, H. P., 27 Pemberton Sq.
Hall, J. R., 4 P. O. Sq.
Halstrom, C. A., 7 Exchange Pl.
Hartwell & Richardson, 68 Devonshire St.
Hatch, F. A., 27 School St.
Hasty, J. A., 68 Devonshire St.
Hill, A. F., 74 Tremont St.
Holmes, Wm., 252 Columbus Ave.
Hurd, W. Frank, 35 Congress St.
Ispen, L. S., 68 Devonshire St.
Kelley, J. T., 57 Mt. Vernon St.
Kelley, Samuel D., 209 Washington St.
Kendall & Stevens, 8 Oliver St.
Kingsbury & Richardson, 43 West St.
Lafield, J. G., 13 Exchange St.
Langdon, J. G., 14 Pembroke St.
Lewis, Edwin, Jr., 9 Park St.
Lewis, W. W., 85 Water St.
Lewis & Paine, 6 Beacon St.
Little, Brown & Moore, 70 Kilby St.

Wm. Hatch & Co.

200 Tremont Street. - - Near Boylston Street.

Boston, Mass.

DESIGNERS, Manufacturers and Gilders of Artistic Picture Frames, also dealers in Art Goods. . . . .

♦

Old Frames Re-gilded.

♦

N. B. It will pay lovers of Antique China to look at our collection.

Lockwood, Greene & Co., 131 Devonshire St.
Longfellow, Alden & Harlow, 6 Beacon St.
Lord & Fuller, 19 Exchange Pl.
Loring & Phipps, Exchange Building, State St.
Lummus, W. W., 48 Congress St.
McFarland, Goodrich & McFarland, 2 Beacon St.
McGinty, J. A., 53 State St.
McGinty, Wm. H., 53 State St.
McKay, H. S., 54 Devonshire St.
McKim, Mead & White, 218 Boylston St.
Metcalf & Hoyt, 50 Bromfield St.
Moffette, Geo., Jr., 34 School St.
Moore, F. H., 27 School St.
Moseley, Herbert, 50 Bromfield St.
Mulcahy, J., 43 Milk St.
Murray, J., 178 Devonshire St.
Newcomb, E. A. P., 5 Pemberton Sq.
Nichols, G. L., 28 State St.
Nudd, Carlos, 12 P. O. Sq.
Ober, J. F., 113 Devonshire St.
Nourse, H. M., 5 Pemberton Sq.
Parker, H., 3 Hamilton Pl.
Peabody & Stearns, 53 State St.
Perkins & Belton, 13 School St.
Peters, Wm. Y., 13 School St.
Phillips, H. A., 53 State St.
Pinkham, A. B., 43 Warren St., Roxbury.
Pope, Fred, 209 Washington St.
Preston, H. J., 104 Water St.
Preston, Wm. G., 186 Devonshire St.
Putnam, J. P., 4 Pemberton Sq.
Quigley, Wm. B., 20 Cobden St.
Rand & Taylor, 28 School St.
Rice, J. H., 79 Milk St.
Richards, J. R., 55 Kilby St.
Richards, Wm. P., 55 Kilby St.
Rinn, J. P., 194 Washington St.
Rodman, W. A., 54 Devonshire St.
Rotch & Tilden, 85 Devonshire St.
Russell, C. A., 46½ Warren St., Roxbury.
Rantin, Samuel, 50 Gurney St.
Rice, F. L., 125 Milk St.
Robbins, Joseph, 22 School St.
Shepherd, A. W., 69 Charlestown St.
Shepherd, F. H., 7 Exchange Pl.
Smith, F. W., 113 Devonshire St.
Spofford, John C., 178 Devonshire St.

JOHN SAMPLE, Jr.

 Designer, Illustrator, and Engraver on Wood.

PROCESS AND HALF-TONE PLATES.

Interior and Exterior Photographer.

27 SCHOOL STREET,
Niles Building.
BOSTON.

Sears, W. T., 70 Kilby St.
Shaw & Hunnewell, 9 Park St.
Shepley, Rutan & Coolidge, 122 Ames Building.
Silloway, T. W., 10 Park Sq.
Smith & Smith, 22 School St.
Smith, O. F., 23 Court St.
Smith, F. H., 144 Boylston St.
Snell & Gregerson, 110 Tremont St
Stephenson, H. M., 3 Pemberton Sq.
Stewart & Binney, 802 Sears Building.
Stickney & Austin, 50 Bromfield St.
Sturgis & Cabot, 19 Exchange Pl.
Thayer, S. J. F., 17 Milk St.
Thayer, George B., 164 High St.
Tracy, Patrick A., 14 State St.
Thompson, S. B., 113 Devonshire St.
Tilden, C., 87 Warren St., Roxbury.
Tobey, S. Edwin, 10 Tremont St.
Untersee, Joseph F., 178 Devonshire St.
VanBrunt & Howe, 35 Congress St.
Vaughan, H., 5 Pemberton Sq.
Vinal & Tracy, 17 Milk St.
Wait & Cutter, 70 Kilby St.
Wakefield, F. M., 120 Boylston St.
Walker & Kimball, 13 Walnut St.
Ware, William Roach, 211 Tremont St.
Warren, H. L., 9 Park St.
Weissbein & Jones, 41 Tremont St.
Wentworth, W. P., 8 Exchange Pl.
West, Albert M., 266 Washington St.
Weston, F. W., 99 Equitable Building.
Wheelwright & Haven, 6 Beacon St.
Winslow & Wetherel, 3 Hamilton Pl.
Woodcock, S. S., 40 State St.
Waterhouse, W. E., 50 State St.
Wilson, E. J., 70 Kilby St.
Zerrahn, F. E., 9 Hamilton Place.

The E. W. Noyes Co.

13 BROMFIELD STREET,
BOSTON.

IMPORTERS AND DEALERS IN

PAINTINGS,
    ENGRAVINGS,
        ETCHINGS AND
            PHOTOGRAPHS.

Artistic Framing, Lowest Prices.

THE E. W. NOYES CO.,
13 Bromfield Street.

Illustrators and Designers.

Aldine Engraving Co., 681 Washington St.
Allen, Fred H. & Co., Stanhope St.
Anshelm, W. J., 94 Boylston St.
Art Publishing Co., 132 Boylston St.
Art Engraving Co., 3 School St.
Atwood, F. G., 53 Boylston St.
Bacon, Francis, 96 Washington St.
Bailey, Miss Amy E., Dudley Pl., Roxbury.
Beal, 3 Winter St.
Bicknell, W. H. W., Winchester.
Blair, C. H., 16 Mount Vernon St.
Boston Engraving Co., 227 Tremont St.
Boston Illustrating Co., 7 State St.
Brandenburg, C. A., 70 Water St.
Brown, M. L., 22 Pemberton Sq.
Burnham, R. A., 9 Milk St.
Burley, John, 103 South St.
Cartwright, W. L., 227 Tremont St.
Chase, F. D., Jr., 48 Winter St.
Clark, Geo. A., 9 Milk St.
Clarke, Fred C., 110 Tremont St.
Copeland, Charles, Studio Building.
Dennison, H. A., 94 Boylston St.
Dillaway, E. S. & Co., 11 Bromfield St.
Desaptes, Etienne, 65 Wareham St.
Dunham, Horace, 66 Clarendon St.
Eastman, A. C., Dedham.
Emerson, C. C., 2 Park Sq.
Flagg, Louis, 9 Park St.
Franklin Engraving Co., 17 Franklin St.
Frizzell & Chaloner, 2 Park Sq.
Gallagher, Sears, 3 Winter St.
Gardner, M. J., 227 Tremont St.
Garrett, E. H., Winchester.
Gonels, Leon F., 145 Dartmouth St.
Goodridge, J. F., 4 Pemberton Sq.
Guild, S. P., 88 Boylston St.
Hallowell, G. H., 356 Boylston St.
Heliotype Printing Co., 211 Tremont St.
Hirshauer, H., 33 Boylston Building.

Artists' Materials.

We are direct importers of all the prominent foreign manufacturers, and can furnish our customers with the best quality of material at the very lowest prices obtainable. Among the many prominent lines that we carry we mention

Winsor & Newton's Oil and Water Colors,
Lacroix Mineral Colors,
Schoenfeld's German Colors.

We also have one of the finest assortments of Artists' Brushes obtainable anywhere. Write for one of our illustrated price lists of artists' materials.

Amateur Photographic Materials.

We are direct representatives of all the prominent makers of Photographic Material, and can furnish full lines of such makers as

E. & H. T. Anthony & Co.
The Scovill & Adams Co.
Eastman Kodak Co.
Rochester Optical Co.

and others of note. We also mention the fact that our assortment of Dry Plates is the largest to be found in Boston. No matter what you need in this line, we can sell it to you at lower prices than can be obtained elsewhere. Three fine electric lighted dark rooms and instruction free of all charge to our customers.

Houghton & Dutton,
Tremont and Beacon Sts.

Hendry, Frank, 196 Summer St.
Howe, J. A., 282 Washington St.
Hub Engraving Co., 27 Boylston St.
Hudson, C. W., 13 Hilton St., Hyde Park.
Jackson, Miss M. A., 2 Park Sq.
Jackson, Robert W., 96 Washington St.
Kaula, William, 145 Dartmouth St.
Kennedy, J. W., 15 Herrick St., Allston.
Kibbe, H. W., 181 Tremont St.
Kilburn & Cross, 433 Washington St.
Kingman, F., 22 School St.
Laskey, H. G., 67 Studio Building.
Low, Gilman, Studio Building.
Lux Engraving Co., 3 Gilbert Pl.
MacDonald, P., 400 Northampton St.
Mann, J. H., 31 West St.
Marsh, Henry R., 328 Washington St.
Meynelle, Louis, 616 Washington St.
Monks, J. A. S., 12 West St.
Moore, E. L., 7 State St.
Murphy, J. P. & Co., 478 Washington St.
Petzold, C. R., 78 Chauncy St.
Poole, Bert, 28 School St.
Proctor, E. L., 7 State St.
Reed, C., 12 West St.
Reed, Miss Ethel, 145 Dartmouth St.
Robinson, L. S., 92 Oliver St.
Richards, Mr., 145 Dartmouth St.
Russell, W., 616 Washington St.
Sample, John, Jr., Niles Building.
Scroff, A., 3 Tremont Row.
Sandham, H., 178 Boylston St.
Shea, P. H., 101 Milk St.
Shepherd, A. W., 69 Charlestown St.
Small, F. O., 31 Pinckney St.
Smith, J. B., Jr., 282 Washington St.
Smith, F. B., 228 Tremont St.
Stuart, Miss Mabel, 69 Brattle St., Cambridge.
Thayer, Miss T., 69 Brattle St., Cambridge.
Tolman, Stacy, Allston, Mass
Upham, W. H., 227 Tremont St.
Wallace, W., 48 Winter St.
Wing, A. F., 145 Dartmouth St.
Wood, W. H., Jr., 22 Walton St., Roxbury.

Hub Engraving Co.

ILLUSTRATIONS FOR . .

BOOKS, PERIODICALS,
NEWSPAPERS, Etc.

By the Photo-Engraving Processes.
In Half-Tone or Relief Plates.

Reproductions of Plans, Maps, Paintings,
Photographs, Wash Drawings, etc.

SPECIAL APPARATUS FOR NIGHT WORK.

Hub Engraving Co.,
27 Boylston Street, - - - Boston, Mass.

Architectural Draughtsmen.

Adden, Willard P., 22 Beacon St.
Alden, Charles H., Hingham.
Aldrich, Will S., 15 Maple Ave., Somerville, Mass.
Atherton, Walter, 87 Milk St.
Barton, George E., 131 Tremont St.
Benier, John W., 1 Walker St., Cambridge.
Bisby, C. W., 3 Hamilton Pl.
Blaney, Dwight, 919 Exchange Building.
Blake, H. L., 186 Devonshire St.
Boone, Allen E., 2 Pemberton Sq.
Bosworth, George F., 87 Milk St.
Bowditch, A. H., 1112 Exchange Building, 53 State St
Brown, Horace, 53 State St.
Brown, W. S., 79 Milk St.
Bubier, A. C., Rangley Park, Winchester, Mass.
Case, John W., 122 Ames Building.
Clark, W. J., 122 Ames Building.
Claus, William, 28 School St.
Coombs, W. M., 68 Devonshire St.
Crockett, G. W., 919 Exchange Building.
Cromack, J. M., 919 Exchange Building.
Dana, Percy E., 932 Exchange Building.
Dean, G. R., Ames Building.
Dow, R. N., Avon Hill St., North Cambridge.
Drew, G. A., 6 Beacon St.
Driver, J. A., 60 Devonshire St.
Dudley, W. N., 89 State St.
Dunham, Charles B., 54 Devonshire St.
Elliott, E. H., 25 Mt. Vernon St.
Ferguson, Frank W., 1110 Exchange Building.
Fernald, George P., 70 Kilby St.
Ford, Lyman A., 8 Beacon St.
Fowler, J. Chandler, 17 Milk St.
Fowler, J. Sumner, 114 Huntington Ave.
Gay, Joseph B., 60 Devonshire St.
Gibbons, Robert W.
Hale, Herbert D., 3 Hamilton St.
Hale, D. C., 122 Ames Building.
Haley, John J., 9 Park St.

AMES ART STORE,

23 BROMFIELD ST.

✣

Castings made to order from Artists' Models. Anything that can be copied or reproduced. . . . . .

✣

Medallions, Panels, Busts and Statuettes from Mythological, Allegorical and Fancy Designs.

Boylston Art Studios,

62 BOYLSTON ST., Cor. Boylston and Tremont Sts.,

BOSTON, MASS.

Mrs. E. HOLLIS, Principal.

Lessons given in
  CHINA, OILS, WATER COLORS, TAPES-
  TRY PAINTING, DRAWING, STILL LIFE
  OR DESIGNING.

All branches taught by competent teachers.

Descriptive circular free upon application.

Hall, John W., 8 Hillside St.
Harding, George C., 27 Doane St.
Hayward, H. C., Rockville Park, Roxbury.
Hill, C. M., 120 Boylston St.
Holt, H. C.
Hooker, Richard, 10 Elmore St., Brookline.
Howe, Wallis E., 6 Beacon St.
Hoyt, W. T. S., 120 Boylston St.
Hoyt, E. H., 50 Bromfield St.
Hutchins, F. H., 60 Devonshire St.
Jones, I. H., 9 Park St.
Jepson, George, 620 Atlantic Ave.
Jepson, John, 219 Tremont St.
Kavanaugh, Jas. F., 69 Chestnut St.
Kendall, Frank A., Framingham, Mass.
Kerr, Wm. G., 2 Ashburton Pl.
Kilham, W. H., 122 Ames Building.
Lane, L. A., 932 Exchange Building.
Lee, J. S., 8 Beacon St.
Little, C. A., 10 Tremont St.
Mack, John, 144 Boylston St.
Maginnis, C. D., City Hall.
Maher, E. F., 87 Milk St.
McGonigle, Harold, 85 Devonshire St.
McLean, W. H., Newton.
Metcalf, P. B., 50 Bromfield St.
Morse, J. F., 53 State St.
Mooney, C. S., 87 Milk St.
Newton, Geo. F., 919 Exchange Building.
Nichols, W. H., 131 Tremont St.
Norcross, F. A., 54 Devonshire St.
Overmire, E. P., Milton, Mass.
Palmer, C. F., 585 E. Fifth St., S. B.
Patch, C. E., 53 Tremont St.
Porter, Geo., 166 Devonshire St.
Pollard, A. A., 32 Whitney St., Roxbury.
Rice, A. W., Jamaica Plain.
Rice, Walter E., 6 Beacon St.
Rogers, E. L., 6 Beacon St.
Ryerson, E. D., 39 Tuttle Ave., Dorchester.
Schrender, O. P., 36 West Cedar St.
Smith, F. P., 113 Devonshire St.
Spencer, R. C., Jr., Ames Building.
Sprague, Arthur C., 186 Devonshire St.
Stone, Geo. W., 122 Ames Building.
Tallant, Hugh, 60 Cedar St., Roxbury.
Tracy, E. P., 14 State St.

INK FOR PEN DRAWINGS,

MECHANICAL AND ARTISTIC.

HIGGINS' AMERICAN DRAWING INKS.

Read what a Great Artist-Draughtsman says about them.

"I might as well give at once the name of the ink I use, and which, of course, I believe cannot be equalled. It is HIGGINS' AMERICAN DRAWING INK. . . . There is no ink equal to it for half a dozen reasons. . . . I know of no other ink for artists that is put up in so sensible a manner. . . . This ink is just as good at the last drop as when you open the bottle. I never knew but one photo-engraver to complain of it. It is jet black, without shine, flows freely, and never clogs the pen. In short, from the time you open the bottle until you have put all its contents on paper you have no reason to find fault with it." — *Jo. Pennell in Pen Drawing and Pen Draughtsmen*, published by Macmillan & Co., London and New York, 1889.

We have never solicited a testimonial, but the genuine merits of the inks have called forth scores of spontaneous indorsements like the above.

The inks are as follows: — **Blacks**, two kinds, **Waterproof**, insoluble when dry, and **General**, soluble.

COLORS. Carmine, Scarlet, Vermilion, Brick-Red, Blue, Yellow, Orange, Green, Brown, Indigo, Violet. These colors are all waterproof and unusually brilliant and permanent. They are rapidly taking the place of cake colors, being always ready, and are much brighter and smoother.

PRICES IN SMALL BOTTLES, 25 CENTS. HALF PINTS, $2.00.

For sale by all Dealers in Artists' Materials and Stationers generally.

CHAS. M. HIGGINS & CO., Mfrs.

168 to 172 Eighth St., Brooklyn, N. Y.

Trowbridge, A. B., 46 Chestnut St.
Tuckertt, C. R., 85 Devonshire St.
Untersee, F. J., John Hancock Building.
Vallance, Hugh, 60 Devonshire St.
Van Stratton, Jacque, 19 Exchange Pl.
Wales, G. C., 919 Exchange St.
Walker, W. L., 60 Devonshire St.
Walsh, T. F., Ellery St., Cambridge.
Wells, W. G., 8 Beacon St.

1835, DANIEL DAVIS, JR. 1849, PALMER & HALL. 1856, THOMAS HALL. 1892, THOMAS HALL & SON.

Thomas Hall & Son,

MANUFACTURING

ELECTRICIANS and OPTICIANS,

MANUFACTURERS AND IMPORTERS OF

Magnetic, Galvanic and Meteorological Instruments, and Philosophical Apparatus,

19 BROMFIELD ST.,

BOSTON.

ARTISTS' REDUCING LENSES, mounted and unmounted. In stock and made especially to order. Something which every artist should have. The small ones are about as large as a medium sized watch, come in chamois-skin cases and are easily carried in the pocket. The large ones are made with metallic frames and wooden handles, protected so that laid down they cannot be scratched. For engravers and draftsmen.

We also manufacture **BLURRING GLASSES**, which are made for blurring paintings, either in oil or water color. Are made the same as above. Samples always in stock, and prices on special work quoted whenever requested. Correspondence solicited.

H. H. CARTER & CO.

PAPER MERCHANTS AND MANUFACTURERS,
ENGRAVERS,
PUBLISHERS, ETC.

♦

CALLING CARDS, WEDDING AND CLASS-DAY INVITATIONS A SPECIALTY.

♦

3 BEACON STREET,

BOSTON.

Art Reference List (Classified).

ARCHITECTS' SUPPLIES.
Frost & Adams, 37 Cornhill.
Hall, Thos. & Son, 19 Bromfield St.
Wadsworth, Howland & Co., 84 Washington St.

ARCHITECTURAL PHOTOGRAPHS.
Dunton, C. H. & Co., 136 Boylston St.
Moulton Photograph Co., Salem, Mass.
Soule Photograph Co., 338 Washington St.

ART BOOKS.
Allen, F. H. & Co., Stanhope St.
Art Publishing Co., 132 Boylston St.

ART GLASS.
Ford & Brooks, Pelham Studios.
Phipps, Slocum & Co., 9 Park St.
Redding, Baird & Co., 83 Franklin St.

ART GLASSES.
Hall, Thos. & Son, 19 Bromfield St.

ART GALLERIES.
Chase, J. Eastman, 7 Hamilton Pl.
Doll & Richards, 2 Park St.
Kimball, Walter & Co., 9 Park St.
Noyes, E. W. Co., 13 Bromfield St.
Williams & Everett, 190 Boylston St.

ARTISTS' MATERIALS.
Carpenter, Woodward & Morton (wholesale), 151 Milk St.
Edmands, C. J., 16 Bromfield St.
Fisher, T. L., 69 Cornhill.
Frost & Adams, 37 Cornhill.
Hall, Thos. & Son, 19 Bromfield St.
Hastings, T. C. & Co., 34 Cornhill.
Hollander, Bradshaw & Folsom, 615 Washington St
Houghton & Dutton, Beacon St., cor. Tremont St.
Meade, Dodge & Co., 4 Park St.
Paige, Mrs. E. M., 74 Boylston St.
Pope, F. J., 36 West St.
Richey's Art Store, 576 Tremont St.
Wadsworth, Howland & Co., 84 Washington St
White, John C., 10 Bromfield St.

ART PHOTOGRAPHS.
Art Publishing Co., 132 Boylston St.
Dunton, C. H. & Co., 136 Boylston St.
Kimball, Walter & Co., 9 Park St.
Moulton Photograph Co., Salem, Mass.
Notman Photographic Co., 3 Park St. and 480 Boylston St.
Soule Photograph Co., 338 Washington St.
Williams & Everett, 190 Boylston St.

ART PHOTOGRAPH PUBLISHERS.
Moulton Photograph Co., Salem, Mass.
Soule Photograph Co., 338 Washington St.

ART PUBLISHERS.
Allen, F. H. & Co., Stanhope St.
Art Publishing Co., 132 Boylston St.

ART SCHOOLS.
Boston Training School of Music, Music Hall Building.
Boylston Art Studios, 62 Boylston St.
Carlson, Emil, 12 West St.
Cowles Art School, 145 Dartmouth St.
Massachusetts Normal Art School, Exeter and Newbury Sts.
New England Conservatory of Music, Franklin Sq.
Rydingsvärd, Karl von, 2 Park Sq.
School of Painting, Art Museum, Copley Sq.

ART STORES.
Ames' Art Store, 19 Bromfield St.
Chase, J. Eastman, 7 Hamilton Pl.
Dunton, C. H. & Co., 136 Boylston St.
Doll & Richards, 2 Park St.
Foster Bros., 164 Boylston St.
Hatch, Wm., 209 Tremont St.
Kimball, Walter & Co., 9 Park St.
Noyes, E. W. Co., 13 Bromfield St.
Soule Photograph Co., 383 Washington St.
Williams & Everett, 190 Boylston St.

ART TEACHERS.
Adams, C. L., 248 Boylston St.
Allen, Miss M. C., Pierce Building.
Bailey, Miss Mercy A., 145 Dartmouth St.
Baker, Mrs. E. A., 62 Boylston St.
Bannister, Mrs. E. M., 180 Columbus Ave.
Barnard, E. H., 23 Irvington St.
Bartlett, Geo. H., 27 Tremont Row.
Bass, Mrs. E. E., 524 Tremont St.
Bennet, Mrs Cecilia, 131 Tremont St.

Benson, F. W., 23 Irvington St.
Blake, Mrs. Alice, Mass. Normal Art School.
Blaney, H. R., 8 Follen St.
Blaney, Mrs. H. Farley, 8 Follen St.
Bradford, Miss M. A., 30 Studio Building.
Brackett, S. L., 616 Washington St.
Branner, J. L., 7 Warren St., Roxbury.
Caldwell, C. W., 180 Tremont St.
Carlson, Emil, 12 West St.
Churchill, W. W., Jr., 23 Irvington St.
Cobb, Cyrus, N. E. Conservatory of Music.
Child, Miss Elizabeth, Art Museum.
Claus, W. A. J., N. E. Conservatory of Music.
Cleaver, Mrs. Florence, 272 Dudley St.
Clerk, W. F., 80 Monroe St., Roxbury.
Crosby, Mrs. H. A., 2 Park Sq.
Cross, Anson K., 145 Dartmouth St.
Dabney, Miss J. P., 37 West Cedar St.
Decamp, Joseph, Mechanics' Building.
Deblois, F. B., 48 Winter St.
Durgin, Miss Harriet, 59 Pierce Building.
Durgin, Miss Lyle, 59 Pierce Building.
Emerson, E. W., Art Museum.
England, C., 27 School St.
Field, Mrs. L. B., 62 Boylston St.
Geer, Miss Grace W., 62 Boylston St.
Goodhue, B. C., 145 Dartmouth St.
Goodwin, Miss Emma F., 2304 Washington St.
Hardwick, M. H., 12 West St.
Hathaway, S. W., 2 Park Sq.
Heath, H. K. M., 207 Shawmut Ave.
Highwood, C., 127 Tremont St.
Hollis, Mrs. E., 62 Boylston St.
Howard, Mrs. May, 3 Temple Pl.
Kaula, W. J., N. E. Conservatory of Music.
Kitson, H. H., 145 Dartmouth St.
Kronberg, Louis, 246 Boylston St.
Langerfeldt, T. O., 129 Charles St.
Leavitt, Miss Agnes, 159 A Tremont St.
Macombie, Eva M., 18 Boylston St.
Major, E. L., 145 Dartmouth St.
Monks, J. A. S., 12 West St.
Moulton, Miss, Hotel Pelham.
Munsel, Albert H., Mass. Normal Art School.
Myrick, Frank, N. E. Conservatory.
Nolen, M. Caroline, 48 Boylston St.
Nowell, Miss A. C., 180 Tremont St.

SPECIMEN HALF-TONE.

THE ALDINE ENGRAVING CO.,   -   681 WASHINGTON STREET.
Wood Engraving, Half-Tone and Photo-Engraving.

Nute, Miss F. Evelyn, 60 Studio Building.
Paine, Mrs. E. A., 5 Cortes St.
Palmer, Miss Adelaide, 149 A Tremont St.
Perrin, Miss Julia, 2 Park Sq.
Plaisted, Miss Z. M., 6 Beacon St.
Pope, Miss Edith, N. E. Conservatory of Music.
Richardson, Miss Ellen A., 57 Pierce Building.
Ruggles, Theo., 145 Dartmouth St.
Rydingsvärd, Karl von.
Sandham, H., 152 Boylston St.
Sanderson, C. W., 20 Beacon St.
Scudder, Miss J. M., 2 Park Sq.
Shyley, Mrs. C. H., 62 Boylston St.
Skowskowski, C. V., 36 Bromfield St
Smith, J. L., Art Museum.
Sprague, 2 Park Sq.
Stone, J. M., 23 Irvington St.
Swift, Mr. C. L., 2 Park Sq
Tarbell, E. C., 23 Irvington St.
Temple, Miss Grace M., N. E. Conservatory of Music.
Tewksbury, Miss Fannie, 212 Boylston St.
Turner, Ross, 212 Boylston St.
Villiers, C. Frederick, 180 Tremont St.
Walker, C. Howard, Art Museum.
Walker, Miss Lilian, 24 Studio Building.
Williams, F. D., 23 Irvington St.
Wood, Mrs. Ann B., 31 Berwick Park.

ARTISTIC PHOTOGRAPHERS.
Art Publishing Co., 132 Boylston St.
Notman Photographic Co., 3 Park St. and 480 Boylston St.

ARTISTIC STATIONERY.
Carter, H. H. & Co., 3 Beacon St.

BLURRING GLASSES.
Hall, Thos. & Son, 19 Bromfield St.

BOOKLETS.
Carter, H. H. & Co., 3 Beacon St.

CAMERAS.
Blair Camera Co., 471 Tremont St.
French, Benj. & Son, 319 Washington St.
Thurston, John H., 50 Bromfield St.

CASTS, MEDALLIONS, ETC.
Ames' Art Store, 23 Bromfield St.

G. P. RAYMOND,

COSTUME PARLORS,

3 Pemberton Square, - - - Boston, Mass.

✣

COSTUMES

.. FOR ..

Masquerades, Old Folks' Concerts, Private Theatricals, Tableaux, Balls, etc.

GILMAN LOW,

ARTIST.

Teacher of Drawing, Painting, Composition and Penmanship.

LADIES' WEDDING AND BALL DRESSES
DESIGNED AT SHORT NOTICE. . . . .

Studio, - - - 87 Studio Building,

110 TREMONT STREET.

✣

Pupil of CHEVALIER TOMMASO JUGLARIS.

✣

What Chevalier Tommaso Juglaris says of Mr. Low: "While under my instruction I found Mr. Low one of my most talented pupils. He has a particular talent for composition, in which he brings out ideas in a very fantastical and imaginative style." CHEVALIER TOMMASO JUGLARIS, Instructor and Member of the Royal Academy of Turin and Florence. Milan, Italy, Nov. 20, 1892.

"You possess a quality in this branch of art that very few have, the talent natural for composition." TOMMASO JUGLARIS.

CHINA DECORATING.

Boylston Art Studios, 62 Boylston St.
Bennet, Miss Cecilia, 131 Tremont St.
Crosby, Mrs. H. A., 149 A Tremont St.
Goodwin, Miss E. F., 2304 Washington St.
Moulton & Barry, Misses, Hotel Pelham.
Perrin, Miss Julia, 2 Park Sq.
Richardson, Mrs. E. R., 57 Pierce Building.
Swift, Mrs. C. L., 2 Park Sq.
Walker, Miss Lilian, 29 Studio Building.

CHINA KILNS.

Walter, T. A. & Co., Hotel Pelham.

CHRISTMAS CARDS.

Carter, H. H. & Co., 3 Beacon St.

COLORED PHOTOGRAPHY.

Art Publishing Co., 132 Boylston St.
Notman Photograph Co., 3 Park St. and 480 Boylston St.

COPPER ENGRAVING.

Allen, F. H. & Co., Stanhope St.
Art Publishing Co., 132 Boylston St.
Notman Photographic Co., 3 Park St. and 480 Boylston St.

COSTUMERS.

Curtis & Weld, 10 Hayward Pl.
Raymond, Geo. P., 3 Pemberton Sq.

DRAUGHTSMEN'S SUPPLIES.

Frost & Adams, 37 Cornhill.
Hall, Thos. & Son, 19 Bromfield St.
Wadsworth, Howland & Co., 84 Washington St.

ENGRAVINGS.

Chase, J. Eastman, 7 Hamilton Pl.
Doll & Richards, 2 Park St.
Foster Bros., 164 Boylston St.
Kimball, Walter & Co., 9 Park St.
Noyes, E. W. Co., 13 Bromfield St.
Williams & Everett, 190 Boylston St.

ELECTRO-TINT PLATES.

Notman Photograph Co., 3 Park St. and 480 Boylston St.

ENGRAVERS.

Aldine Engraving Co., 681 Washington St.
Allen, F. H. & Co., Stanhope St.
Andrew, John & Son Co., 196 Summer St.
Art Publishing Co., 132 Boylston St.

SPECIMEN HALF-TONE.

SUFFOLK ENGRAVING CO.,
235 WASHINGTON ST.,
BOSTON.

Bartlett, E. S., 421 Washington St.
Bates, Thomas S. & Co., 29 Avon Pl.
Becker, August, 55 Oliver St.
Berry, Andrew C., 12 West St.
Berry, J. & J. & Co., 68 Cornhill.
Bird, M. T. & Co., 23 West St.
Blagdon, John S. & Co., 11 Bromfield St.
Bolton, J. B., 383 Washington St.
Boston Engraving Co., 227 Tremont St.
Boston Illustrating Co., 7 State St.
Boynton, G. W., 425 Washington St.
Brett, Wm. H., Engraving Co., 30 Bromfield St.
Bricher, H. W. & Co., 3 School St., room 6.
Briggs, Albert W., 370 Washington St.
Briggs, Wm. P., 24 Winter St.
Brigham & Co., 131 Summer St.
Brown, C. F., 179 Washington St.
Brown, Nathan, 22 School St., room 18.
Bugbee, Albert V., 265 Washington St., room 6.
Callahan, M. T., 30 Bromfield St.
Carpenter, Reuben, 30 Bromfield St.
Carter, H. H. & Co., 3 Beacon St.
Clapp, George W., 357 Washington St.
Coburn, C. S. Co., 34 Bromfield St.
Coleman, Edward H. N., 179 Washington St.
Copeland, C. G., 42 Court St., room 32.
Dunbar & Chapin, 74 Tremont St.
Dunlop, Frank P., 235 Washington St.
Eaton, Henry M., 3 School St., room 7.
Eberhardt, A., 2 Province Ct.
Engraving, G. & P. Co., 58 Federal St.
Farmer Bank Note Co., 38 Pearl St.
Farrington, C. E. & Co., 620 Atlantic Ave.
Fitzgerald, William E. & Co., 427 Washington St. (plates).
Fowle, E. A., 22 Pemberton Sq.
Franklin Engraving Co., 17 Milk St.
Geib, G. A., 196 Summer St.
Gilbert, Marcus H., 3 Winter St.
Graves & Green, 302 Washington St. (wood).
Hartshorn, J. F., 421 Washington St.
Hedge, F., 14 State St., room 46 (wood).
Heliotype Printing Co., 211 Tremont St.
Holland & Heintz, 409 Washington St.
Hooker, W. J., 62 Sudbury St.
Hopkins, C. W., 339 Washington St.
Hub Engraving Co., 27 Boylston St.
Johnson & Thompson, 31 Milk St.

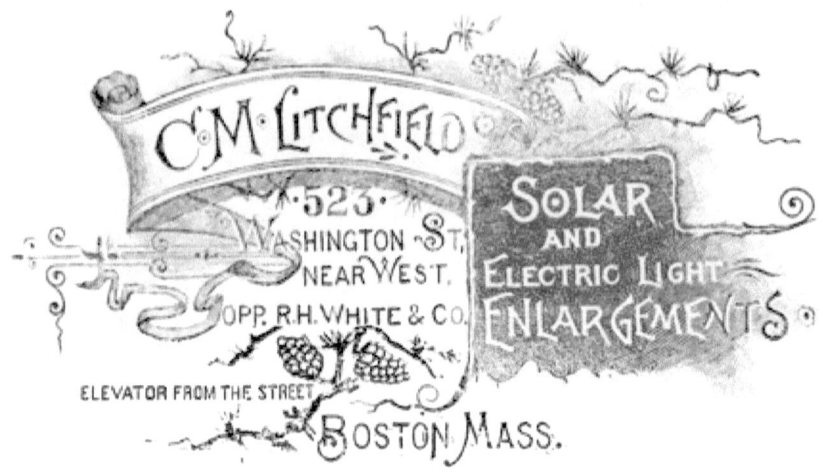

BROMIDE ENLARGEMENTS A SPECIALTY.

Silver Medal awarded by the Massachusetts Charitable Mechanic Association, 1892.

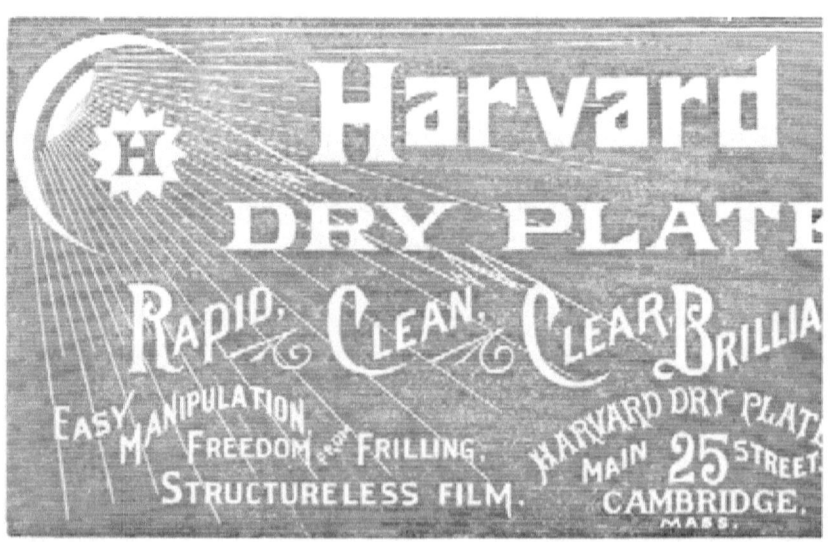

Kilburn & Cross, 433 Washington St.
Lowell, John A. & Co., 147 Franklin St.
Lux Engraving Co., 3 Gilbert Place.
Matthews, George H., 12 School St.
Mitchell, A. W., 200 Washington St.
Mitchell, Charles F., 42 Court St.
Mitchell, Henry, 110 Tremont St.
Pfan, Louis P., 25 F. H. Sq. (wood).
Photo-Electro Engraving Co., 275 Washington St.
Popp, H. & Co., 41 Essex St.
Power, J. E., 15 Cornhill.
Reilly, Joseph B., 57 Washington St.
Remick, H. E., 216 Washington St.
Robinson Engraving Co., 32 Hawley St.
Russell, Harry L., 329 W. Broadway.
Russell & Richardson, 41 Temple Pl.
Sargent Engraving Co., 19 Temple Pl.
Scamman, J. B., 345 A Washington St.
Scott, J. D., 144 A Tremont St.
Snow, Henry H., 12 West St., room 1.
Spenceley, Frederick, 51 Franklin St.
Stockwell, F. F. 99 Court St.
Stuart, F. T., 42 Court St.
Suffolk Engraving Co., 235 Washington St.
Sylvester, H. E., 54 North St.
Taylor, A. B., 58 Winter St.
Twitchell, Charles A. & Co., 31 Cornhill.
Walker, Charles A., 42 Court St.
Webster, E. Ambrose, 7 Exchange Pl.
Whittemore, J. M. & Co., 26 School St.
Wilcox, J. A. J., 22 Pemberton Sq.
Williams, Frank H., 22 Pemberton Sq.
Wittkoff, T. F. 125 Tremont St.
Young, Joseph D., 425 Washington St.

ENGRAVERS' SUPPLIES.
Sellers, Alfred, 58 Fulton St., N. Y.

ETCHINGS.
Kimball, Walter & Co., 9 Park St.
Williams & Everett, 190 Boylston St.

ETCHERS.
Art Publishing Co., 132 Boylston St.
H. R. Blaney, 8 Follen St.

FOREIGN PHOTOGRAPHS.
Dunton, C. H. & Co., 136 Boylston St.
Kimball, Walter & Co., 9 Park St.
Williams & Everett, 190 Boylston St.

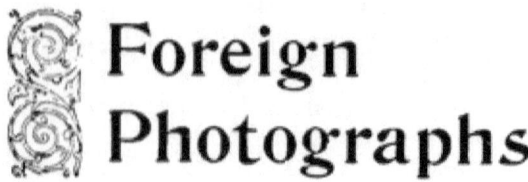

Foreign Photographs

. . . of the .

VIEWS, PAINTINGS AND SCULPTURE

OF THE OLD WORLD.

Imported direct in all sizes, . .

. . Mounted and unmounted.

LARGEST STOCK IN AMERICA
OF BRAUN'S CARBONS. . . .

Mounting and Framing to order.

Catalogue of 10,000 Subjects on application.

C. H. DUNTON & CO.

136 Boylston Street, - - Boston.

FOREIGN PHOTOGRAPHS.
(DIRECT IMPORTERS.)

Dunton, C. H. & Co., 136 Boylston St.

FRAME MAKERS.

Allerton, Wm., 143 Columbus Ave.
Amolsky, L., 156 Richmond and 269 Hanover St.
Beckford, D. C., 43 Winter St.
Bigelow & Jordan, 56 Summer St., room 19 (manufs.).
Bennett, Charles R., 85 State St.
Bissell, Richard L., 12 West St., room 20.
Bornstein, L., 92 Prince St.
Boston Art Co., 35 Hanover S .
Boston Frame and Moulding Co., 80 Beverly St.
Braun, E. B., 6 Charlestown St.
Braun, G. J., 16 Beverly St.
Braun, H. W., 25 Beverly St.
Brewster, Wm. A., 101 Leverett St.
Brodie E. L. & Co., 33 Doane St.
Brown, Harry W., 1317 Washington St.
Brown, T. A. & C., 72 W. Broadway.
Cabot, Joseph F. & Bro., 89 Sudbury St.
Cass, H. N. (estate), 175 Hanover St.
Chase, J. Eastman, 7 Hamilton Pl.
Chisla & Braissoli, 28 Kneeland St.
Cohn, L. & Co., 18 Charlestown St.
Conant Bros. & Bragg Co., 73 Union St.
Costello, John, 13 Battery St.
Curtin, Daniel, 106 Warrenton St.
Dennis, F. H., 338 Washington St.
Doll & Richards, 2 Park St.
Dugan, E. P., 383 Main St.
Dunton, C. H. & Co., 136 Boylston St.
Eastern Frame Co., 90 Portland St.
Enwright, M. J., 132 Main St.
European Portrait Co., 33 W. Canton St.
Fardy, Nicholas, 493 Swett St.
Fielding, A. A., 104 Dorchester St.
Firth, P. W., 13 Meridian and 15 Lewis St., E. B.
Folsom, George C., 36 Bromfield St., room 48.
Foster Brothers, 164 Boylston St.
Friedland, Hermann, 1437 Tremont St.
Friedlander, R., Mrs., 1934 Hanover St.
Frost & Adams, 37 Cornhill.
Furlong, N., 469 Tremont St.
Gans, Joseph, 33 Beach St.
Golden, John, 26 Green St.

Miss E. S. BADGER,

Manufacturer and Dealer in

Umbrellas, Parasols and Canes,

29 TEMPLE PLACE.

One easy flight or Elevator.

Parasols to order to match costumes. Lamp Shades to order in size, color or style desired. Repairing and re-covering.

E. J. GOULD & CO.

Mats and Passepartouts,

25 BROMFIELD STREET,

Room 14,

BOSTON.

Interior Decorator and Furnisher. - - - -

Miss LILLIAN WALKER,

Original Designs in Tapestry Painting - - - - - - and Embroideries.

Special exhibition of choice Embroideries and Paintings from October to June.

Room 41, 110 Tremont St., Boston, Mass.

PHOTOGRAPHIC PRINTING

OF EVERY DESCRIPTION
KODAK WORK DEVELOPING ETC
ALBUM MOUNTING (THIN PAPER)
A SPECIALTY

S. M. TAYLOR

ROOM 94, 70 KILBY ST. BOSTON MASS. MASON BLD'

BRANCH AND PORTRAIT STUDIO,

41 CENTRAL AVENUE, LYNN.

Gould, E. J., 25 Bromfield St.
Hastings & Davenport, 8 Hamilton Pl.
Hatch, William & Co., 209 Tremont St.
Heller, Isaac L., 63 Maverick Square.
Hemmenway, E. S. Co., 166 North St.
Hollyer, A., 168 Lincoln St. (mounter).
Horgan, Robey & Co., 34 Bromfield St.
Hubbard, F., 8 Bromfield St.
Kihlgren, C. A., 339 Washington St.
Kimball, Walter & Co., 9 Park St.
Knell, Fred G., 44 Warren St., Roxbury.
Latimer, J., 6 Chardon St.
Lemos, Frederick, 58 Prince St.
Lewis & Cohen, 61 Hanover St.
Lombard, J. N., 288 Boylston St.
Lonergan, J. J., 47 Hanover St.
Margolsky, H., 168 Hanover St.
McCabe, James, 207 Havre St.
McKenney & Connorton, 22 Bromfield St.
McNamara, John J., 11 Bromfield St.
Meleney, H. Seward, 245 Main St.
Merrow, C. E. A., 521 Washington St., room 26.
Morrill, A. W., 17 Broadway Extension.
Moulton, B. S. & Co., 42 Hanover St.
New England Portrait Co., 103 Milk St., room 14.
Nichols, Richard, 614½ Bromfield St.
Norman, T. W. & Co., 44 Bromfield St., and 116 Eliot St.
Noyes, E. W. Co., 156 Boylston St.
O'Brien, John J., 69 Cornhill.
Pope, Frank J., 36 West St.
Restein Charles, 810 Washington St.
Rhodes, Clinton & Co., 8 Medford St.
Richey, R. & W. W., 576 Tremont St.
Rodgers, H. T., 63 Charlestown St.
Rumney & Grohe, 103 Meridian St., E. B.
Smith Bros., 20 and 22 Bromfield St.
Smith, Eben, 182 Lincoln St.
Sprague & Hathaway Company, 12 Studio Building.
Strater, F. J., 353 Washington St. (passe-partouts).
Trainer, F., 1 Cottage Pl., Roxbury.
Van Auken, J. H., 505 Washington St.
Ward, Charles F. & Co., 8 Charlestown St.
Waters, I. G. & Co., 10 Canal St. (dealers' supplies).
Whelan, Jeremiah F., 1603 Washington St.
Willard, J. H., 50 Green St.
Williams & Everett, 190 Boylston St.
Zack & Halpern, 61 Leverett St.

NOTMAN PHOTOGRAPHIC CO.
480 BOYLSTON STREET,
3 PARK STREET.

JOHN GREENLEAF WHITTIER

THE BEST STUDIO IN BOSTON FOR FANCY DRESS AND ALL STYLES OF PHOTOGRAPHS.

SPECIAL RATES TO ARTISTS.

FRENCH COLOR PROCESS.
Art Publishing Co., 132 Boylston St.

LENSES.
Hall, Thomas & Son, 19 Bromfield St.
French, Ben. & Son, 319 Washington St.
Thurston, John H., 50 Bromfield St.

INTERIOR DECORATOR.
Walker, Miss Lillian, Studio Building.

MATS.
Gould, E. J., 25 Bromfield St.

MEZZO TINTS.
Notman Photographic Co., 3 Park St. and 480 Boylston St.

OIL PAINTINGS.
Eastman, Charles J., 7 Hamilton Pl.
Doll & Richards, 2 Park St.
Kimball, Walter & Co., 9 Park St.
Noyes, E. W. Co., 13 Bromfield St.
Williams & Everett, 190 Boylston St.

PANELS.
Gould, E. J., 25 Bromfield St.

PASSE-PARTOUTS.
Gould, E. J., 25 Bromfield St.

PHOTO-ENGRAVERS.
Aldine Engraving Co., 681 Washington St.
Allen, F. H. & Co., Stanhope St.
Andrew, John A. & Son Co., 193 Summer St.
Art Publishing Co., 132 Boylston St.
Boston Engraving Co., 227 Tremont St.
Boston Illustrating Co., 7 State St.
Franklin Engraving Co., 28 School St.
Hub Engraving Co., 27 Boylston St.
Lux Engraving Co., 3 Gilbert Pl.
Photo-Engraving Co., 67-71 Park Pl., New York.
Suffolk Engraving Co., 235 Washington St.

PHOTO-GELATINE PROCESS.
Allen, F. H. & Co., Stanhope St.
Art Publishing Co., 132 Boylston St.
Notman Photographic Co., 3 Park St. and 480 Boylston St.

PHOTOGRAVURES.
Allen, F. H. & Co., Stanhope St.
Art Publishing Co., 132 Boylston St.

LARGE PHOTOGRAPHS

..FOR..

Schools, Colleges, and Halls of Private Residences.

These photographic enlargements, ranging in size from three to eight feet in length, are reproduced from imported photographs of ancient and modern art and subjects of architectural and historic interest. They are so treated that they can be framed with or without glass, and are now being adopted by many schools for decorating walls and for educational purposes, and are presented as class pictures by graduating classes. This is in answer to the many inquiries for LARGE, INEXPENSIVE pictures of subjects that cannot be obtained in any other way.

WM. H. PIERCE & CO.

352 Washington St., - - Boston, Mass.

SOLAR ENLARGEMENTS.

Photographic Supplies
OF ALL KINDS.

Detective Cameras
OF ALL KINDS.

All the latest
PRINTING PAPERS.

ALBUMS
Of every description.

Especial care given to arranging and mounting prints with gelatine in albums or on cards.

Developing and Printing.

Dark Room for changing Plates.

JOHN H. THURSTON,

50 BROMFIELD ST. (up One Flight), Room **6**
BOSTON, MASS.

Elson, A. W. & Co., 176 Oliver St.
Heliotype Printing Co., 209 Tremont St.
Rogers, John S., John Hancock Building.
Wheeler, J. H., 299 Washington St.

PHOTO-LITHOGRAPHIC PROCESS.

Art Publishing Co., 132 Boylston St.

PHOTOGRAPHERS.

Notman Photographic Co., 3 Park St. and 480 Boylston St.

PHOTOGRAPHIC APPARATUS — MATERIALS.

Barker & Starbird, 59 Bromfield St.
Blair Camera Co., 471 Tremont St.
Boardman, A. F., 57 Bromfield St.
French, Benj. & Son, 319 Washington St.
Hall, Thomas & Son, 19 Bromfield St.
Harvard Dry Plate Co., Main St., Cambridge.
Horgan & Roby, 62 Bromfield St.
Houghton & Dutton, Tremont St., Cor. Beacon St.
Koebler, Chas., 18 Province St.
Stall, W. W., 509 Tremont St.
Thurston, John H., 50 Bromfield St.
Washburn, D. C., 13½ Bromfield St.

PHOTOGRAPHIC MOUNTING.

Thurston, John H., 50 Bromfield St.

PHOTOGRAPHIC PRINTING.

Taylor, S. M., 70 Kilby St.

RUGS.

Hapkok, Bogigian & Co., Beacon St. cor. Park St.
Torrey, Bright & Capen, 348, 350 Washington St.

SOLAR PRINTING.

Art Publishing Co., 132 Boylston St.
Litchfield, C. M., 581 Washington St.
Pearce, W. H. & Co., 352 Washington St.

STATUARY.

Alberti, V., 191 Shawmut Ave.
Caponi, 12 Province Court.
Daprato, A. & Company, 13 Waverly Block, Charlestown.
Garibaldi, Pietro, 51 Kneeland St.
Giannotti, P., 110 Warrenton St.
Nardi, J. & Company, 145 Charlestown St.

TEACHER MODELLING IN CLAY.

Rydingsvärd, Karl von., 2 Park Sq.

Harold Fletcher,

 Portraits in Oil and Restorer of Paintings,

Wednesdays, Thursdays and Saturdays.

149 A TREMONT STREET, BOSTON.

Mrs. E. E. Bass

 Receives Pupils in Drawing and Painting at her Studio,

524 Tremont St., — Boston.

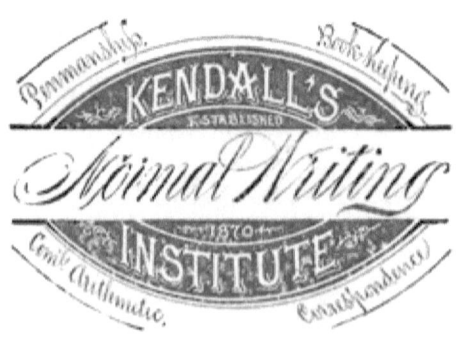

TEACHER OF MANUAL TRAINING.

Rydingsvärd, Karl von, 2 Park Sq.

WATER COLOR.

Chase, T. Eastman, 7 Hamilton Pl.
Doll & Richards, 2 Park Sq.
Kimball, Walter, 9 Park St.
Noyes, E. W. Co., 13 Bromfield St.
Williams & Everett, 190 Boylston St.

WATER COLOR PAINTERS AND TEACHERS.

Allen, Miss M. C., Pierce Building.
Blaney, Mrs. H. Farley, 8 Follen St.
Flagg, H. Peabody, 54 Studio Building.
Goodwin, Emma F., 2304 Washington St.
Hathaway, Miss, 2 Park Sq.
Leavitt, Miss Agnes, 159 Tremont St.
Monks, J. A. S., 12 West St.
Nowell, Miss Annie C., 180 Tremont St.
Nute, Miss F. Evelyn, 110 Tremont St.
Perrin, Miss Julia, 2 Park Sq.
Sanderson, Chas. H., 20 Beacon St.
Scudder, Mrs. J. M., 2 Park Sq.
Sprague, Julia A., 2 Park Sq.
Swift, Mrs. C. L., 2 Park Sq.
Tewksbury, Miss Fannie W., 212 Boylston St.
Turner, Ross, 248 Boylston St.
Walker, Miss Lilian, Studio Building.
Williams, F. D. 23 Irvington St.

WOOD CARVING.

Rydingsvärd, Karl von, 2 Park Sq.

WOOD ENGRAVERS.

Art Engraving Co., 3 School St.
Brown, M. L., 22 Pemberton Sq.
Bunter, Alonzo, 6 Beach St.
Chandler, Victor L., 43 Milk St.
Conant, J. S. & Co., 3 Franklin St.
Dillaway, E. S. & Co., 11 Bromfield St.
Hedge, F., 14 State St.
Learned, B. E., 38 Pearl St.
Murphy, J. P. & Co., 478 Washington St.
Pfau, Louis P., 25 Faneuil Hall Sq.
Sample, John, Jr.
Stockin, Arthur, Niles Building, 3 School St.
Taylor, J. L., 157 Washington St.

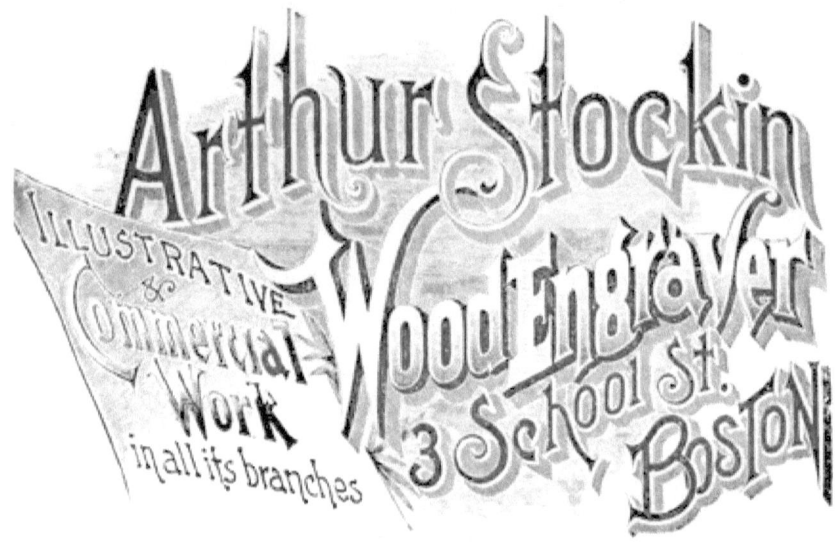

· FOR ALL ILLUSTRATIVE PURPOSES ·
PROCESS DRAWING

BOYLSTON BUILDING · 18 BOYLSTON ST · ROOM 59
BOSTON

ZINC ETCHINGS.

Allen, F. H. & Co., Stanhope St.
Aldine Engraving Co., 681 Washington St.
Andrew, John & Son Co., 183 Summer St.
Art Publishing Co., 132 Boylston St.
Boston Illustrating Co., 7 State St.
Franklin Engraving Co., 28 School St.
Hub Engraving Co., 27 Boylston St.
Suffolk Engraving Co., 333 Washington St.

Index.

	Page		Page
Architects	84	Gould, E. J. & Co.	114
Architectural Draughtsmen	95	Hall, Thomas & Son	100
Art Clubs and Associations	27	Harvard Dry Plate Co.	116
Art Educational Institutions	45	Hatch, William & Co.	86
Art Exhibitions	41	Higgins, C. M. & Co.	98
Art Institutions, United States	7	Hollander, Bradshaw & Folsom	76
Art Institutions and Collections, Boston	21	Houghton & Dutton	92
		Hub Engraving Co.	94
Art Reference List (classified)	101	Kimball, Walter & Co.	Bet. 40, 41
Art Scholarships	50	Kromberg, Louis	68
Art Stores	10	Knowlton, Miss H. M.	66
Art Tariff	53	Lansil, W. F.	66
Artists, Represented at Columbian Exposition	65	Litchfield, C. M.	110
		Leavitt, Miss Agnes	68
Artists' Studio Addresses	67	Low, Gilman	100
Illustrators and Designers	94	Lux Engraving Co.	Opposite Index
Law of Copyright	58	Monks, J. A. S.	74
Aldine Engraving Co.	Bet. 104, 105	Moulton Photograph Co.	102
Allen, F. H. & Co.	Frontispiece	N. E. Conservatory of Music	6
Allen, Mrs. M. C.	72	Notman Photograph Co.	116
Ames' Art Store	86	Nowell, Miss A. C.	74
Art Publishing Co.	Bet. 62, 63	Nute, Miss F. E.	74
Badger, E. S.	114	Pearce, W. H. & Co.	118
Bass, Mrs. E. E.	120	Perrin, Miss J.	72
Bennett, Miss Cecilia	68	Raymond, G. P.	106
Blaney, H. R.	80	Richardson, Mrs. E. A.	68
Blaney, Mrs. H. F.	80	Richey's Art Store,	Inside back cover
Boston Illustrating Co.	Bet. 48, 49	Rydingsvärd, Karl von	68
Boylston Art Studios	96	Sample, J., Jr.	88
Brackett, S. L.	72	Sanderson, G. W.	74
Brown, M. L.	Opposite inside front cover	Scudder, Miss J. M.	68
		Seavey, G. W.	74
Caldwell, C. W.	70	Sellers, Alfred	84
Carlson, Emile,	Inside back cover	Soule Photograph Co.	Inside front cover
Carter, H. H. & Co.	100		
Churchill, W. W., Jr.	66	Sprague, Miss J. A.	72
Cowles' Art School	78	Stockin, A.	122
Clarke, Fred C.	72	Strain, D. J.	66
Da Prato, A. & Co.	82	Suffolk Engraving Co.	108
Dennison, H. A.	122	Swift, Mrs. C. L.	72
Dunton, C. H. & Co.	112	Taylor, S. A.	114
E. W. Noyes Co.	90	Tewksbury, Miss Fannie W.	66
Ennéking, J. J.	68	Thurston, J. H.	118
Flagg, H. P.	66	Turner, Ross	66
Fletcher, Harold	120	Villiers, C. F.	72
Foster Bros.	64	Wadsworth, Howland & Co.	64
Franklin Engraving Co.	Bet. 56, 57	Walter, T. F.	80
Frizzel & Chaloner	88	Walker, Miss Lillian	70, 114
Frost & Adams	70	Williams & Everett,	Opp. Preface
Goodwin, E. P.	74	Williams, F. D.	74

www.ingramcontent.com/pod-product-compliance
Lightning Source LLC
Chambersburg PA
CBHW020058170426
43199CB00009B/327